SOPWITH
Company Profile 1912-1920

THE SPIRIT OF SOPWITH

I f it had not been for the ungrateful manoeuvre by the British Government to introduce the 'Excess War Profits Duty' after the First World War, the name of Sopwith within the British aviation industry could have potentially lived on until the 1970s. Tommy (later Sir Thomas) Sopwith would not have been forced to liquidate the successful Sopwith Aviation Company in 1920 and the name would have continued through the inter-war, Second World War and post-war period removing the future Hawker and Hawker Siddeley names from aviation history. While the likes of the Sopwith Hurricane does not quite have the same ring to it, it was the same group of people who had created the company that continued on to form H G Hawker Engineering, named after Australian-born test pilot Harry Hawker. Tommy Sopwith went on to become the chairman of Hawker Siddeley right up to his retirement and would remain a consultant with British Aerospace until 1980; by then aged 92!

The aviation bug took hold of Sopwith in 1910 when he witnessed John Moisant carry out the first passenger flight across the English Channel on August 17. Wasting no time, Sopwith taught himself to fly in a Howard Wright Avis Monoplane; taking to the air for the first time on October 22 only to crash after a mere 300 yards. Undeterred, Sopwith persevered and on November 22 was awarded Royal Aero Club Aviation Certificate No.31. Flying success soon followed in competitions and in June 1912 Sopwith, Fred Sigrist and several others formed the Sopwith Aviation Company, basing their new enterprise at Brooklands. Like all fledgling aviation companies of the period, it was a tough start but success in competition followed and by the outbreak of the First World War the company began to thrive. Military orders had been received by Sopwith since late 1912, but now expansion was essential. Unable to cope alone, substantial sub-contracts were issued to William Beardmore, Clayton & Shuttleworth, Fairey and Ruston & Proctor, to name but a few. At its peak the Sopwith organisation employed over 5,000 people and went on to produce 16,000 aircraft during its eight year history, obviously the bulk of these on the back of war contracts. Some of the company's machines became household names, such as the Pup, 1½ Strutter, Triplane, Camel, Dolphin and Snipe, the latter serving a much-reduced post-war RAF until the late 1920s.

The spirit of Sopwith definitely remained in every Hawker and later Hawker Siddeley product right up to the Harrier, which was built in the same Canbury Works in Ham that produced hundreds of Snipes in 1918. Sir Thomas Octave Murdoch Sopwith passed away on January 27, 1989, just nine days after his 101st birthday.

One of the few original Sopwith aircraft to survive is G-EBKY, a 'Pup' operated by the Shuttleworth Collection, at Old Warden in Bedfordshire. This aircraft was one of the last ten Pups to be built and was actually completed as a two-seat Dove for civilian use. It was acquired by Richard Shuttleworth in the 1930s and converted back into Pup configuration before debuting at the 1938 Royal Aeronautical Society Garden Party. Today it wears the markings of RNAS Pup 9917, a Beardmore built aircraft that was fitted with Le Prieur rockets when it served aboard the seaplane carrier HMS Manxman. *Darren Harbar*

Credits/Bibliography W Green & G Swanborough (The Complete Book of Fighters); H King (Sopwith Aircraft 1912-1920); P Lewis (British Aircraft 1809-1914); F Mason (British Bomber since 1914); B Robertson (Sopwith – The man and his aircraft); O Thetford (Aircraft of the RAF since 1918); O Thetford (British Naval since 1912) & *Flight* magazine.
Proof Reading Steve Bridgewater & Jamie Ewan. **Design and Layout** Rob Terry.

Publisher and Managing Director Adrian Cox. **Executive Chairman** Richard Cox. **Commercial Director** Ann Saundry. **Group Editor** Nigel Price.
Distribution Seymour Distribution Ltd +44 (0)20 7429 4000. **Printing** Warners (Midlands) PLC, The Maltings, Manor Lane, Bourne, Lincs PE10 9PH.
ISBN 978 1 910415 82 5

Published by Key Publishing Ltd, PO Box 100, Stamford, Lincs PE19 1XQ.
Tel: +44 (0) 1780 755131. Fax: +44 (0) 1780 757261. Website: *www.keypublishing.com*

CONTENTS

The Sopwith Snipe was the last rotary engine powered fighter to serve in the RAF and was only completely replaced in 1927 by the radial engine powered Gloster Grebe. This example is an exact reconstruction of Snipe F2367 and wears the markings of 70 Sqn. The real F2367 which was on occupational duties in Germany immediately post-war. This flying replica was built by the New Zealand-based company The Vintage Aviator Ltd and is operated in the UK by the WW1 Aviation Heritage Trust at Stow Maries, Essex. *Darren Harbar*

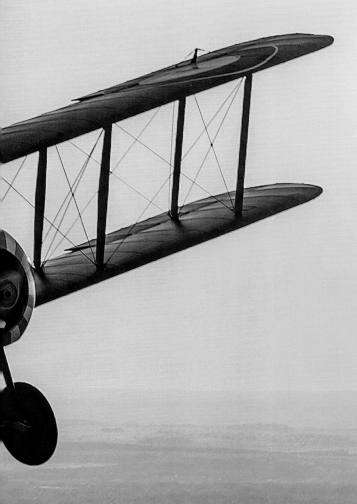

TOMMY'S DOGFIGHTERS OF THE FIRST WORLD WAR

Sopwith designs played a crucial role in the ultimate Allied victory over the Western Front

Tom Sopwith founded the Sopwith Aviation Company in 1912, having first become involved in flying two years previously after ventures in motoring, yachting and ballooning. His former mechanic, Fred Sigrist, proved an able works manager, while the first company draughtsman, R J Ashfield, was eventually to become project engineer. From Australia came test pilot Harry Hawker, whose demonstration of the Company's first aircraft, the Tabloid single-seat biplane, made a profound impression on the crowds at Hendon, the aviation centre of the day. Hawker attracted two other Australians to the works; Harry Kauper, who was to design a machine gun interrupter and Bert Hinkler, who was later to achieve world renown for his epic long distance flights.

Sopwith 1½ Strutters were built as two-seat fighters and single-seat bombers. Both variants saw service with 3 Wing, RNAS; the pioneers of strategic bombing when the unit attacked Luxeuil-les-Bains in 1916.
Key Collection

Trophy-Winning Tabloid

Hawker sailed back to his homeland in 1914 with a Tabloid to enthral crowds at the Melbourne and Sydney racecourses. Meanwhile, back in Europe Sopwith's Company attained its crowning pre-war success, the winning of the Schneider Trophy Contest of 1914 held at Monaco on April 20. This was achieved by converting a Tabloid to seaplane configuration to meet the requirements for this international maritime aircraft contest. In Hawker's absence, Howard Pixton had been selected to pilot the first aircraft, the first of British design to enter this contest.

Much was expected of Sopwith aircraft when war came. The Royal Flying Corps (RFC) regarded the Tabloid as a suitable scout, while the Royal Naval Air Service (RNAS) was anxious to obtain large numbers of the fastest seaplanes in the world. Contracts were placed, aircraft were built and the Tabloid entered service. However, all was not well. Tabloids had not been designed for war; they had a limited capacity for a war load and, being light, they suffered from the rough landing grounds in France and frequently ground-looped or overturned. The RNAS used a flight of Tabloids based in Belgium to bomb German airship sheds, but the

aircraft had to be destroyed or abandoned to the advancing enemy early in the war.

The Schneider floatplanes, with wing-warping control, proved difficult to fly, suffered from frequent engine failure, and could only take off from calm water. Fitted with a single Lewis gun they were allotted to coastal stations for standby duty against Zeppelin attacks but, in the half-hour it took for them to reach the height flown by German airships, there was little chance of interception. Schneiders were also seen as coastal patrol aircraft but their endurance was often limited by headwinds, particularly when light bombs were carried on anti-submarine patrols. Taken to sea to act as spotters for the light cruisers and destroyers of the Harwich Force, the type embarked on seaplane carriers and lighters anchored out in the North Sea as defence outposts waiting to combat Zeppelins, but every effort to utilise them seemed doomed to failure.

The effects of sea spray on their 100hp Gnome Monosoupape engines rendered them notoriously unreliable. If there was a slight swell, they were likely to capsize with broken float struts. On one occasion three Schneiders broke up in succession after being hoisted out from carriers to take off to attack a Zeppelin. The Company designed a sturdier version with normal aileron control surfaces and powered by an 110hp Clerget engine. Named the Baby, production took place at that company's works in Leeds leading to the type also being referred to as the Blackburn Baby.

An early foray by Baby floatplanes was a Harwich Force operation in which a seaplane carrier sent off two Short Seaplanes with two of the new Sopwiths to seek out and bomb airship sheds on the island of Sylt. All the seaplanes were lost except one Baby, whose pilot failed to find the sheds at Sylt but discovered Zeppelin sheds at Tondern. He dived low over this target, but in spite of repeated attempts his bombs failed to drop.

Imagining that such ill fortune could not prevail, units of the Harwich Force escorted the seaplane carriers HMS *Vindex* and *Engadine* to a position off Sylt on May 3, 1916. Eleven Schneider and Baby floatplanes were hoisted out, to take off to bomb the recently-located Tondern airship station. As the engines were being started, attendant destroyers protectively circled the stationary carriers, creating such a wash that one Baby immediately capsized, four others broke propellers and spray choked the engines of three others. Of the three which successfully rose from the water, one was brought down within seconds by fouling the aerial of a destroyer, while another descended within minutes with engine trouble. A single Baby reached the target area, only to find it covered with mist.

In the Aegean Sea, the Schneiders were more successful and did useful work observing gunfire. Final production Baby floatplanes with a 130hp Clerget engine proved more reliable and made regular patrols from coastal stations around the British Isles and the Adriatic approaches. With unrestricted U-boat warfare from April 1917, anti-submarine patrolling became their main task. Both the Fairey and Parnall companies were asked to produce similar small seaplanes to the basic Sopwith pattern. Late in 1918 a number of Baby floatplanes were acquired by the US Navy base at Killingholme, Lincolnshire and four were sent to the United States for evaluation.

First Fighting Aircraft

The Sopwith two-seater, colloquially known as the 1½ Strutter due to its unusual wing strut arrangement, was the Company's first true fighting aircraft. It was armed with a Vickers gun firing through the propeller arc by means of the Kauper-Sopwith gun gear operated by the pilot, while the observer in the rear cockpit wielded a Lewis gun on a universal mounting. After reaching the RNAS in April 1916, the RFC pressed for similar aircraft required for the coming Battle of the Somme. Teething troubles with engine and gun stoppages were gradually overcome. A single-seat bomber version was produced and these became some of the first strategic bombers with the Royal Navy's 3 Wing in eastern France, carrying four 65lb bombs each to targets in the Ruhr.

Thomas Octave Murdoch Sopwith, pioneer aviator, circa late 1880s. *Key Collection*

Impressed by both versions and influenced by the use of a French 130hp Clerget engine, the French Air Service equipped some 70 escadrilles in 1917-18 with licence-built aircraft. In all, over 4,200 were manufactured in France for the French and Americans, while the Sopwith factory at Kingston built 246 and other British contractors, produced some 900. In 1918, after some 1½ Strutters had been relegated for training in Britain, some were converted as naval spotter aircraft for shipborne use.

The first of the Sopwith single-seat fighters, the Pup, came onto the Western Front with the 1½ Strutter in 1916. A prototype of the Pup, also known as the Sopwith Scout, was tried out over the Front in May; it was September, however, before 1 Wing RNAS, received the aircraft and the first RFC Pups reached the Front on December

24. Both air arms were delighted with the manoeuvrable biplane, which could out-turn contemporary German aircraft. In spite of the relatively low-powered 80hp Le Rhone engine, the Pup had a good ceiling, giving its pilots the advantage of height, an important factor in gaining superiority over adversaries.

Five RNAS and three RFC squadrons operating Pups at the Front brought Sopwith aircraft once more to the fore. The Pups were utilised to the full and up to four light bombs were carried for strafing attacks. It was with the Pup that the RFC started regular offensive patrolling, normally starting with a dawn patrol. For balloon strafing, eight electrically-fired Le Prieur rockets could be fitted to the wing struts.

As a naval aircraft fitted with flotation bags, the Pup was used by the RNAS in coastal defence and as a shipborne aircraft for spotting and anti-Zeppelin work. They were accommodated aboard warships on platforms placed above gun turrets, take-off being achieved by accelerating along a ramp sitting along the gun barrels. This method proved effective on August 21, 1917 when Flt Sub Lt B A Smart took off from HMS *Yarmouth* following an airship sighting report. After gaining height, Smart intercepted Zeppelin *L23* and shot it down in flames.

Deck Landing Success

Deck landing was another facet of the Pup's pioneer work. Sqn Cdr E H Dunning made the first ship landing on August 2, 1917 after taking off from HMS *Furious* and landing back on the 226ft foredeck while she steamed into wind. The

Pup was partly arrested by a deck landing party who grabbed at toggle ropes hanging from the fuselage and lower wing. On a third attempt to repeat this success, the Pup veered overboard when a tyre burst and the gallant Dunning was drowned. Nevertheless experiments continued with Pups at Isle of Grain, Kent using a synthetic deck and introducing arrestor wires.

The Pup's contemporary, the Triplane, was a revolutionary design. By using three wings, each plane had reduced chord and the pilot enjoyed better visibility than in a conventional biplane. With good manoeuvrability, a decent rate of climb and a respectable top speed of 117mph, the Triplane was a formidable fighter by 1916 standards. The prototype first flew at Brooklands on May 30, 1916 and within minutes of take-off Harry Hawker had looped it three times. In mid-June the prototype was flown to the Front and shortly after its arrival was taking off to intercept an enemy aircraft. This one aircraft, flown aggressively by Flt Lt R S Dallas, gave the Germans the impression of a Triplane squadron in action months before the first squadron became operational early in 1917. Apart from one used experimentally by the RFC, the Triplane was exclusive to the RNAS, however a few Triplanes were supplied to France and one was shipped to Russia, while another went to the United States.

Among the famous pilots who flew Triplanes was Raymond Collishaw, who scored most of his 60 victories flying Sopwith types and was ranked third in the list of leading British and Commonwealth aces. While a single Vickers gun synchronised to fire through the propeller arc

Fred Sigrist, who Tommy Sopwith described as one of the best engineers he had ever known. Sigrist worked with Sopwith from 1910 and following the demise of the company, and after a well-earned break he formed Reid and Sigrist in 1927. *Key Collection*

was standard armament, a few Triplanes were equipped with a twin Vickers arrangement. As with other Sopwith aircraft types, however, the chief faults were with gun stoppages. The Triplane achieved fame out of all proportion to the limited numbers built: 152 saw service, of which two survive, one each in Britain and Russia.

A Sopwith Tabloid with gun and deflector propeller. Lt T Warner and WO J G Brownridge devised this mounting and other installations were made on the side of the fuselage. *Key Collection*

The Formidable Camel

R J Ashfield left the Sopwith Company early in 1918 and Herbert Smith, who was then heading the drawing office, became responsible for design at a time when the most famous of the firm's fighters was evolving as the Sopwith F1. The most significant feature of this fighter was its twin Vickers machine guns at a time when a single gun was normal. Placed atop the engine cowling, at pilot's-eye-level, the guns gave the aircraft a slightly humped appearance, earning it the name Camel.

Ordered for the RNAS, the first Camels reached the Western Front in July 1917 to replace the Pups of 3 and 4 (Naval) Squadrons. Meanwhile, 70 Squadron RFC discarded its 1½ Strutters in favour of Camels; the build-up of Camel squadrons along the Western Front started by re-equipping existing units and continued with new squadrons forming in Britain.

Initially, the Camel was not a success. There was the usual trouble with gun stoppages, the inevitable engine troubles and a dangerous tendency to spin, which caused many fatal accidents. The Camel's success, once the gun gear and ammunition belt feed difficulties had been resolved, was its firepower and manoeuvrability due to its sensitive controls. Once a pilot had the measure of its vices, he became a formidable adversary.

The Camel's performance varied according to the engine fitted; its average maximum speed was 118mph at low level, slightly less at height. The 110hp Clerget engine fitted to the prototype changed to a 130hp Clerget for most Camels in RFC service. Those retained in Britain for home defence generally had a 110hp Le Rhone engine. The Camels with the best performance were those powered by a 150hp BR1 engine, initially exclusive to the RNAS. This engine, originally the AR1 (Admiralty Rotary No.1), was renamed after its designer, W O Bentley.

By the late summer of 1917 until the end of the war, Camels had a profound effect on air operations over the Western Front by regular offensive patrols and strafing attacks. This was emphasised by the official communique for September 19, 1917, a day on which strong

> ## A PATROL OF FOUR CAMELS OF 70 SQUADRON WENT OUT IN THE MORNING TO ATTACK GROUND TARGETS WITH MACHINE GUN FIRE AND BOMBS

winds and low cloud precluded large-scale air operations. 'Flt Sub Lt A R Knight, 8 (Naval) Squadron attacked an Albatros two seater, which he forced to land in a field, apparently much damaged ... A patrol of four Camels of 70 Squadron went out in the morning to attack ground targets with machine gun fire and bombs. Second Lt Stuart attacked a column of about 600 infantry and later dropped two 20lb bombs on targets in Houthulst Forest. Second Lt Quigley attacked several strong points and dropped bombs on two of them. On his way home he fired at troops and shot into communication trenches in the vicinity. Pilots of 10 (Naval) Squadron also did similar work, and

Flt Cdr Saint dropped two bombs in Houthulst Forest where an explosion was caused and then fired 350 rounds into enemy transport along the Staden Road and completely disorganised it ...'

It was this strafing role which led to the Camel TF1 (Trench Fighter No.1) project for an armoured Camel fitted with downward-firing guns. It was soon appreciated that guns placed to fire downward would not have the scything effect of low-level attack by its normal guns. To compensate for the weight of armour, however, a more powerful aircraft was needed.

During the German spring offensive of 1918, the Camels played a vital part both in strafing the advancing German troops and in meeting the increased opposition in the air. By that time Camels were also operating with 28, 45 and 66 Squadrons in Italy opposing the Austro-Hungarian air arm. On this Front Lt A Jerrard won the Victoria Cross after a fight on March 30, 1918 in which he shot down an Albatros and went on with his flight to attack an Austrian airfield. When his comrades were attacked by superior numbers of enemy aircraft, he fought tenaciously in their defence until his Camel was riddled with bullet holes. Finally, with the controls partially shot away, he was forced to land and surrender.

During the intensive fighting of March and April 1918 two pilots of 43 Squadron flying Camels, Captains J L Trollope and H W Woollett, both shot down six enemy aircraft in a single day. Earlier, on the night of January 25, two 44 Squadron pilots flying Camels on home defence duty, Captain G H Hackwill and Second Lieutenant C C Banks, closed on a German Gotha bomber approaching London. Their combined fire-brought the aircraft down to achieve the first victory made at night by direct combat between aeroplanes. There was a growing need for night defence of the British base areas in France, for which night-flying Camel squadrons were formed in 1918. The first, 151 Squadron, reached France on June 21. Among its 16 victories at night was a five-engined Zeppelin-Staaken R.XIV bomber; the squadron also made night strafing attacks on enemy airfields. Altogether the Camel was credited with shooting down 1,294 enemy aircraft.

A shipborne version, officially called Ship's Camel, came into service late in 1917. Designated Camel 2F1 by the Sopwith Company, it differed slightly in dimension, was armed with a single Vickers above the engine cowling and a Lewis gun on the top wing and was powered exclusively by the BR1 engine. The rear fuselage was detachable for stowage and air bags were fitted in the fuselage for flotation in the event of ditching. Ship's Camels were allotted to ships of the Grand Fleet down to light cruisers, replacing Ship's Pups and extending the carriage of fleet fighters to some 40 ships which had a complement of up to three each. The US Navy also acquired Ship's Camels and, on March 9, 1919, they launched their first Camel from the USS *Texas*.

Camels also made the first carrier-borne fighter strike on July 19, 1918 when seven 2F1s rose from the deck of HMS *Furious*, each carrying two light bombs to attack the Tondern airship sheds. Despite a successful strike, a direct hit starting fires destroying the German naval Zeppelins L54 and L60, all of the Camels were lost. However, it was not expected that the aircraft would land back on the carrier's decks. The pilots of the two Camels which ditched were saved by the Fleet and three others were interned after landing on Danish soil.

A total of 5,497 standard Camels were built plus 250 Ship's Camels; of these aircraft, the Sopwith Company built only about ten per cent. The main Camel contractors were Ruston Proctor of Lincoln and Boulton & Paul of Norwich; eight

A Sopwith Pup of 3 Sqn RNAS. The squadron was commanded by Canadian Redford 'Red' Mulock and was placed at the disposal of the RFC in the lead-up to the Battle of Vimy Ridge. *Key Collection*

other firms also built Camel airframes in lesser numbers.

The Sopwith 5F1 Dolphin, appearing while the Camel was in production, was powered by a 200hp Hispano engine. An unusual feature of this single-seat biplane was that the top wing was level with the top of the cockpit, in a design attempt to give the pilot a clear all-round view above; this necessitated moving the bottom wing forward to achieve the correct centre of gravity. This was also an attempt at producing a multi-gun fighter, for in addition to two forward-firing fixed Vickers machine guns firing through the propeller arc, Lewis machine guns could be fitted to the top wing to fire forwards and upwards outside the arc; four light bombs could also be carried.

Approved by the Sopwith Experimental Department on May 23, 1917, the Ministry of Munitions was sufficiently impressed to give Sopwith their largest order to date for 500 Dolphins. Output started late in 1917 and in the New Year 19, 23, 79 and 87 Sqns were flying Dolphins on the Western Front. In spite of the initial engine troubles which dogged all new Sopwith aircraft and pilots discarding their Lewis guns to improve performance, the Dolphin proved equal to both the rigours of the Front and

the attentions of the German fighters. Sopwith, helped by the firms of Darracq and Hooper, built over 1,500 Dolphins by the Armistice.

Snipe and Salamander

The 7F1 Snipe was a direct follow-on from the Camel in design and production. While featuring the same twin-Vickers firepower, its 230hp BR2 engine and double-bay wings made it a more powerful and larger aircraft. A maximum speed of 121 mph was not a great improvement, but its rate of climb and endurance gave the Snipe superiority over the Western Front. Large orders were placed with the Sopwith Company, which had recently acquired new premises at Ham, near Kingston, Surrey. The armoured strafing role, for which the Camel TF1 had been considered, was met by an armoured version of the Snipe named the TF2 Salamander. At the expense of endurance, fuel capacity was reduced to compensate for the weight of armour plate protecting the cockpit. As the Salamander was also ordered from Sopwith in quantity, the Snipe was widely contracted out.

The Snipe started to replace the Camel in service with 43 and 208 Squadrons Royal Air Force and 4 Squadron Australian Flying Corps. How effective these new fighters were is exemplified by the laconic communiqué of the 80th Wing for October 29, 1918: 'A squadron patrol consisting of 15 machines [Snipes] of 4 AFC north-east of Tournai observed a formation of ten Fokker biplanes [D.VIIs] attacking an RE.8. Dived after the EA [enemy aircraft] and in the stern combat that ensued, destroyed eight machines and drove down two out of control. No casualties occurred on our side.' But for the Armistice that November, the Snipe would have become the supreme fighter of the First World War. As it was it became the RAF's standard fighter in the immediate post-war years.

Simultaneously, Sopwith had a variety of experimental aircraft on test in 1918. Their Bulldog 2FR2 two-seat fighter was abandoned after failing to show a marked improvement over the Bristol F.2B Fighter already in service. An armoured two-seat infantry contact patrol aircraft, the Buffalo 3F2, reached the Front for trial in September, too late for its recommended modifications to be incorporated. Like other manufacturers, Sopwith was interested in

One of a batch of 25 Triplanes built by Oakley & Co. of Ilford, the story of N5912 is quite a remarkable one. Originally delivered to Hendon on October 19, 1917 the aircraft joined the War School at Manston and 2 Fighting School Marske during 1918. After many more moves the aircraft finally settled back at Hendon in October 1971 where it remains to this day. *Key Collection*

First delivered to the RAF in June 1918, the Cuckoo was one of the earliest land based torpedo bombers which remained in service until 1923.
Key Collection

utilising the 360hp ABC Dragonfly engine. Prototypes built for this engine were the Snark high-altitude single-seat fighter and the Snapper conventional biplane for the same role. Due to a hold-up in Dragonfly production neither type progressed beyond the experimental stage.

Had the war continued the torpedo-carrying aeroplane would have come into its own. Early Sopwith experiments with torpedo-carrying seaplanes had led to limited production orders but no operational successes. Late in 1916 the Admiralty approached Sopwith about a torpedo-carrying landplane and by mid-1917 the firm had a prototype designated T1 (Torpedo plane No.1) flying. Admiral Beatty had evolved a plan for a mass attack from carrier-borne T1s on the German High Seas Fleet. Taking off as they approached the German coast, the aircraft were to fly in low to torpedo the enemy ships, using their four-hour endurance to fly back to Britain.

The Blackburn works at Leeds were given the production task, helped by two firms which had no previous experience with aircraft. The T1, later renamed the Cuckoo, was further delayed by an Air Board decision to change the 200hp Hispano of the prototype to the 200hp Sunbeam Arab for production. By late 1918, deliveries were made

to 185 Squadron at Gosport working up for the carrier HMS *Argus*, while *Furious* already had Cuckoos aboard for trials at sea.

Transatlantic Failure

In an attempt to sustain a reputation for record-breaking after the war, there was a Sopwith entry for the 1919 Schneider Trophy. This racing seaplane, powered by a 450hp Cosmos Jupiter, had the misfortune to damage its floats during the contest and was beached to prevent it sinking. Repaired and mounted on wheels, it was entered as the Sopwith Rainbow in the 1919 Aerial Derby.

A more ambitious project was the first non-stop Atlantic crossing attempt by Hawker in a specially-built Sopwith aircraft appropriately named the Atlantic. The aircraft was based on the earlier Sopwith B1 single-engined bomber prototype, with a deeper fuselage to accommodate additional fuel for the 360hp Rolls-Royce Eagle engine. It was shipped out to St Johns, Newfoundland to make a west-east air crossing, taking advantage of the prevailing westerly winds.

At dawn on May 18, 1919 Hawker took off with Lt Cdr K K Mackenzie-Grieve as navigator.

After being forced to ditch, Hawker and his comrade were picked up by a Danish cargo vessel, not fitted with wireless, leaving the rest of the world to wait five days for news of their survival.

The Atlantic design was pursued by Sopwith to provide the aircraft for Australian airmen, returning to their homeland, to bid for the Australian Government's ten thousand pound prize. The conditions were that they would fly to Australia within 30 days in an aircraft of British or Commonwealth design. Named the Wallaby the aircraft set out on October 21, 1919, but it was damaged in a landing in Iran. By the time it was repaired it was too late to continue. However, it was utilised in the Commonwealth on mail routes and a similar aircraft, the Antelope, was shipped out from the Sopwith works for the same duty.

Only one twin-engined Sopwith type was built, the Cobham fighter reconnaissance and bomber triplane, on which development continued until 1920. Two monoplane Sopwiths existed; the first, known as the Scooter, had a Camel fuselage fitted with a parasol wing. It was flown by Harry Hawker from mid-1918 and by others until 1926. The second, the Swallow, also utilised a Camel fuselage and was a high-wing monoplane used for experimental work until the end of the war and then discarded.

Sopwith Aviation marketed a two-seat sports version of the Pup after the Armistice, aptly named Dove; ten examples were built. A new design, the two-seat Grasshopper tourer, did not advance beyond a prototype; its contemporary, the Gnu, was built with a cockpit for the pilot and a cabin for two passengers and became the most successful of the post-war Sopwith types. Unfortunately, the Gnu's production run of eleven for British buyers and two for Australian was not sufficient for the company to thrive in the post-war market. With no large-scale orders in the offing, the company closed on September 3, 1920. ❖

Three RAF squadrons were equipped with the Sopwith Snipe before the Armistice, which remained as the standard fighter until 1927.
Key Collection

The Sopwith modified Burgess-Wright biplane at Brooklands. *Flight*

>> **MAY 2, 1912**
First flight using
Green engine

>> **MAY 17, 1912**
Maiden flight with
A.B.C. engine

>> **JUN 8, 1912**
Aircraft wins the
Shell Speed Trophy
at Hendon

American Purchase

A reconstruction of the Burgess-Wright biplane, the Sopwith-Wright Biplane, was bought by Tommy Sopwith during his tour of America in 1911. Fred Sigrist carried out the bulk of the reconstruction work at Brooklands and a report by *Flight* magazine stated that there was virtually nothing left of the original machine however the same configuration remained intact.

The Sopwith-Wright Biplane had twin-pusher propellers, two bay wings and additional interplane struts to which were mounted the propeller shafts. The front spars were positioned along the leading edge of the wing while the rear spar had flexible overhanging sections which were used for warping control. The tail booms were closely spaced and carried twin narrow-chord rudders which were mounted on pivots to the booms. The tailplane tapered to a point while the rear section served as an elevator thanks to its flexibility. A pair of square panels was positioned below the upper mainplane directly in front of the middle interplane struts.

Mounted on the lower middle section and offset to port was the 35hp Green engine with the pilot and passenger accommodated to starboard within a nacelle with a fuel tank positioned directly behind. The propellers were driven by chains, the starboard one crossing over so that they would contra-rotate. The radiator was positioned on the starboard middle strut and the oil tank was mounted above the engine.

The Biplane had a pair of skids for its undercarriage to

> **❝ THE PROPELLERS WERE DRIVEN BY CHAINS, THE STARBOARD ONE CROSSING OVER SO THAT THEY WOULD CONTRA-ROTATE ❞**

which were attacked a pair of triangular 'blinkers' which served to provide extra surface area to improve directional stability. The skids were extended rearwards so that they could support the tail and the lengthy tail booms. To the skids were mounted two pairs of wheels featuring rubber springs. The control system was of the Farman type with a control lever and rudder bar rather than the traditional Wright system. The same Farman control system was installed in the Burgess-Wright variant by Burgess himself on the request of Tommy Sopwith.

The Sopwith-Wright Biplane first flew with a 35hp Green engine on May 2, 1912. Additional successful flights took place the following day and on May 5 the aircraft was entered into the Cross Country Handicap. Flown by F P Raynham, the Biplane finished in third place. Not long after, the Green engine was replaced by a 40hp ABC and with this unit the Biplane first flew on May 17. The Biplane was entered into a number of competitions including the Shell Speed Trophy at Hendon on June 8 which was won by Raynham. Even with these competitive successes the Biplane spent the bulk of its flying career as an instructional trainer at the Sopwith School of Flying. The aircraft's crowning glory came on October 24, 1912. With Harry Hawker at the controls, the Biplane was flown for 8 hours 23 minutes, a new British duration record which also took the prize of the 1912 British Empire Michelin Trophy No.1 and a cash prize of £500.

TECHNICAL DATA
SOPWITH-MODIFIED
BURGESS-WRIGHT

ENGINE: One 35hp Green or one 40hp ABC

WING SPAN: 38ft 9in

LENGTH: 29ft 6in

WING AREA: 475 sq/ft

WING GAP: 5ft 3in

CHORD: 6ft 3in

This biplane, which seated two passengers side-by-side in the front cockpit and the pilot in the rear cockpit, appeared at the same time as the Bat Boat in 1913. It was adopted by both the Naval and Military Wings of the RFC, and at the outbreak of war in 1914 the RNAS had two, Nos.103 and 104. *Flight*

First Sopwith Aviation Co Aircraft

Outstanding among the new aeroplanes exhibited at the 1913 Olympia Aero Show was the Three-seater, the first of the long series of Sopwith tractor biplanes. Designed by Sopwith and Sigrist, the machine represented a distinct advance towards rational and practical aircraft and, together with its Avro and Bristol contemporaries, played its part in establishing the classic British formula which was adhered to for the next two decades.

The Three-seater (dubbed the Hybrid because it combined Wright wings with a new-build fuselage) carried its complement of two passenger's side-by-side in the front cockpit below the centre-section of the wing, the pilot occupying a separate cockpit immediately to the rear. A praiseworthy feature of the design was the provision, on each side of the fore-fuselage, of three large celluloid panels for improved downward vision. The main undercarriage consisted of a pair of normal vee-struts combined with two skids embodying a small wheel at the front of each. Unusual was the fitting of twin tail-skids the width of the fuselage apart. The two-bay wings were slightly staggered and had warping tips, but no fin was installed.

After its emergence, the 80hp Gnome Three-seater

> **II TWO WEEKS LATER, ON JUNE 16, HAWKER TOOK ONE PASSENGER UP TO 12,900FT AND LATER ON THE SAME DAY REACHED 10,600FT WITH TWO PASSENGERS ON BOARD II**

was straightaway demonstrated at flying meetings by H G Hawker, Sopwith's test pilot. On Whit-Monday, 1913, the machine came first in the Cross-country Race at Brooklands and was then taken by Hawker to a height of 7,500ft in 15 minutes. Thereafter, the same pilot proceeded to demonstrate the aircraft's capabilities with several record-breaking climbs. At Brooklands on May 31, 1913, he went to a new British solo height of 11,450ft. Two weeks later, on June 16, Hawker took one passenger up to 12,900ft and later on the same day reached 10,600ft with two passengers on board. On July 27, Hawker and three passengers ascended to 8,400ft. Later in the year he used a modified version fitted with a 100hp Green engine for attempts on the British Michelin Cups Nos.1 and 2, but without success.

The Three-seater was ordered by the RFC, followed by the RNAS, a total of nine being delivered for Service use. These were normally flown as two-seaters only, some of them being aileron-equipped, and the small wheels on the skids were omitted on a few. The Service machines differed also in having rudders of a modified outline. Before the outbreak of war, 5 Squadron, RFC, was flying Three-seaters, and they were employed later by Commander Samson's Eastchurch Squadron and for coastal patrol from Great Yarmouth.

TECHNICAL DATA
SOPWITH THREE-SEATER

ENGINE: One 80hp Gnome

WING SPAN: 40ft

LENGTH: 29ft 6in

WING AREA: 397 sq/ft

EMPTY WEIGHT: 1,060lb

GROSS WEIGHT: 1,810lb

MAX SPEED: 73.6 mph

CLIMB RATE: 400ft in 5.1min

SERVICE CEILING: 12,900ft

>> **JULY 4, 1912**
Maiden flight of 'Hybrid'

>> **MAY 31, 1913**
British solo height record at Brooklands

>> **FEB-AUGUST, 1914**
Service with 5 Sqn, RFC

Bat Boat No.1 with modified twin rudders and the RNAS
serial, No.118 in 1913. *Owen Cooper Collection*

Britain's First Successful Amphibious Aircraft

>> **1913**

Aircraft appears at Olympia

>> **JUN 1913**

Mk IA delivered to Calshot

>> **JUL 8, 1914**

Hawker wins Mortimer Singer award in Mk I

>> **JUL 1914**

Takes part in Spithead Naval Review

>> **AUG 24, 1914**

No.118 begins patrols from Scapa Flow

>> **APR 1915**

Last example withdrawn by the RNAS

BAT BOAT MK I & IA

The Sopwith Bat Boat first appeared at the 1913 Olympia Aero Show, alongside its Three-seater. It was an advanced design for the day and most significantly was the first successful British flying-boat. Initially fitted with a 90hp Austro-Daimler engine, driving an 8ft 6in Levasseur propeller, the Bat Boat was a good-looking machine with pleasing lines thanks to its cedar-planked hull made by Saunders and Company.

The Bat Boat had side-by-side seating with the cockpit being located ahead of the lower wings. With the exception of the hull, all construction was carried out by Sopwith in its Kingston-upon-Thames factory, where each aircraft was assembled. The wings were un-staggered and positioned above the hull and attached to it by two pairs of struts. The Bat Boat had a single rudder and lateral control was achieved by wing-warping. An additional/auxiliary elevator was positioned on the nose of the hull.

The Bat Boat was re-engined with a 100hp Green engine, driving an increased 11ft diameter propeller, so that it could compete in the all-British amphibian category for the £500 Mortimer Singer prize. To qualify as an amphibian, a pair of forward-retracting wheels was installed, so the Bat Boat could operate as a landplane. Other modifications included, twin rudders and a one-piece elevator. Two substantial struts were fitted from the engine to the front of the hull in place of the original wire bracing. Cable-connected ailerons were also installed making this variant considerably

more refined than the original aircraft. Harry Hawker flew the Bat Boat in this form on July 8, 1914 to win the Mortimer Singer prize and not long after, the aircraft was delivered to the Admiralty.

Operated by the RNAS from Calshot, in service, the 90hp Austro-Daimler engine was re-installed and the retracting undercarriage was removed. A searchlight was installed in the nose and the serial No.118 applied. This aircraft took part in the Spithead Naval Review in July 1914 and at the beginning of the First World War was patrolling from Scapa Flow. The aircraft saw service from August 24 but was wrecked on November 21, 1914 in a gale. A second aircraft (serial No.38) also served the RNAS and was similar to the original design.

BAT BOAT MK II

A bigger and improved version of the original 1913 Bat Boat made its debut during the Aero Show at Olympia in 1914. Power was provided by a 200hp Salmson 14-cylinder engine, cooled by a large radiator mounted between the middle-section struts. The general arrangement remained the same but was scaled up, the wings alone being increased by 14ft to 51ft in span by the installation of an extra half-bay combined with braced upper-wing extensions.

Another version was powered by a 225hp Sunbeam engine and was entered for the 1914 *Daily Mail* Circuit of Britain race. Howard Pixton was to fly the aircraft in the race but the outbreak of the First World War prevented it from taking place.

A Salmson-powered Bat Boat pictured during trials on the Solent. *Owen Cooper Collection*

TECHNICAL DATA - BAT BOAT MK II

ENGINE: One 200hp Salmson 2M7	**EMPTY WEIGHT:** 2,300lb
	GROSS WEIGHT: 3,120lb
WING SPAN: 54ft	**MAX SPEED:** 70 mph
LENGTH: 36ft 6in	**CLIMB RATE:** 500ft in 2.5min
WING AREA: 600 sq/ft	**ENDURANCE:** 4hr 30min

The only Sopwith exhibit at the 1914 Aero & Marine Exhibition at Olympia was the new Bat Boat with a 200hp Canton Unne (Salmson) engine. *Flight*

The first Bat Boat with a 100hp Green engine, pictured flying over the Solent. *Flight*

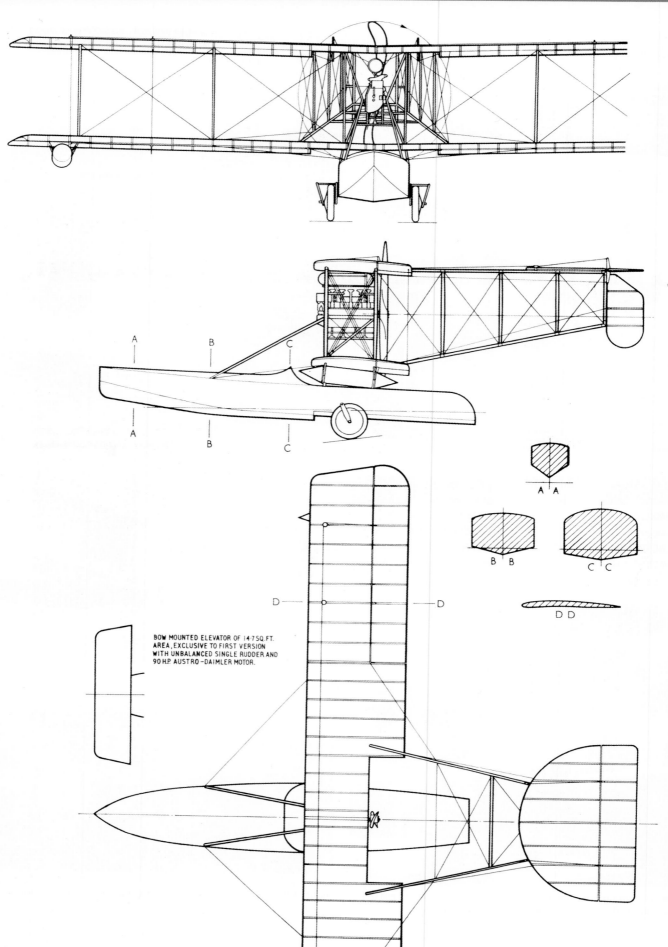

A A

B B   C C

D D

A — A
B — B
C — C
D — D

BOW MOUNTED ELEVATOR OF 14·7 SQ. FT.
AREA, EXCLUSIVE TO FIRST VERSION
WITH UNBALANCED SINGLE RUDDER AND
90 H.P. AUSTRO-DAIMLER MOTOR.

AVIATION SPECIALS

RAF BATTLE OF BRITAIN MEMORIAL FLIGHT
Spectacularly celebrates the Flight's activities and achievements.

£5.99 inc FREE P&P*

VALOUR IN THE AIR
A comprehensive salute to some of the greatest pilots ever take to the skies.

£6.99 inc FREE P&P*

SPITFIRE 80
Tribute to Britain's greatest fighter and possibly the best known combat aircraft in the world.

£5.99 inc FREE P&P*

VULCAN
A tribute to the most challenging and complex return-to-flight project ever.

£3.99 inc FREE P&P*

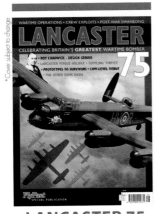

LANCASTER 75
Pays tribute to all who built, maintained and flew Lancasters, past and present.

£5.99 inc FREE P&P*

SCALE MODELLING MOSQUITO
Celebrates with five full model builds, type histories, kit/decal/accessory listings and exclusive scale drawings.

£5.99 inc FREE P&P*

GULF WAR
A must-have for those seeking to understand the conflict that changed the shape of warfare.

£3.99 inc FREE P&P*

RAF OFFICIAL ANNUAL REVIEW 2017
Behind the scenes insight into the aircraft, equipment and people of one of the world's premier air forces.

£5.99 inc FREE P&P*

AVIATION SPECIALS

ESSENTIAL reading from the teams behind your **FAVOURITE** magazines

HOW TO **ORDER**

 OR

PHONE
UK: 01780 480404
ROW: (+44)1780 480404

FREE Aviation Specials App

Simply download to purchase digital versions of your favourite aviation specials in one handy place! Once you have the app, you will be able to download new, out of print or archive specials for less than the cover price!

IN APP ISSUES **£3.99**

Sqn Cdr Spencer Grey's 100hp Sociable in 1914.

» **MAR 1914**
Grey takes Sociable to 10,600ft

» **MAR 25, 1914**
Aircraft damaged at Eastchurch

» **SEP 22, 1914**
Sociable attacks airship shed in Cologne

TECHNICAL DATA
SOCIABLE

ENGINE: One 100hp Gnome Monosoupape

WING SPAN: 36ft

LENGTH: 24ft 3in

EMPTY WEIGHT: 960lb

GROSS WEIGHT: 1,640lb

MAX SPEED: 90 mph

ENDURANCE: 3hr

RNAS Trainer

The Sociable, so called because the crew were seated side-by-side rather than in tandem, was ordered by the British Admiralty for use as a training aircraft by the RNAS. An early passenger was First Lord of the Admiralty Winston Churchill and afterwards it gained the nickname the 'Sopwith Churchill'. Unlike the Tabloid two-seater, the Churchill had two-bay wings, staggered, and carrying inversely-tapered ailerons. The fuselage was long and slender, thus giving the aeroplane an overall resemblance to an Avro 504, notably by reason of the long lever-arm afforded for the 'comma'-form balanced rudder. There was no fin, and the landing gear was of the twin-wheel/twin-skid type that was common on Tabloids. The 80hp Gnome engine originally fitted was later replaced by a 100hp Gnome Monosoupape, though at what stage is uncertain. By March 1914, it does seem sure, however, that the number 149 had been painted on the rudder; and by this time also Sqn Cdr Spenser Grey, flying solo, had taken the machine to 10,600ft.

Clearly, here was an aeroplane fit for military service, and this it was to see in September 1914, crewed, in particular by Spenser Grey and Lt Newton Clare. Dates and details of raids at this period are difficult to determine with absolute accuracy; but that Spenser Grey 'lost' a bomb from No.149 seems well-founded.

In the *Aeroplane*, CG Grey (no relation to Spenser) related the circumstances which followed 149's return to Antwerp in the following terms: 'When Spenser Grey and Newton-Clare landed they saw a vacant space in the pipe-rack which showed that one of the bombs had vibrated itself off. They only hoped that it had fallen in Germany and not in Belgium.

'After dinner they were sitting in the lounge of their hotel when an excited Belgian staff-officer dashed in and told them that a complaint had come from the Dutch Government that one of the Allied aeroplanes had dropped a bomb in the city of Maastricht, and had blown up a school and some houses and had killed a lot of women and children, and that the Dutch Government were seriously contemplating declaring war on Belgium. Spenser Grey turned to Newton-Clare and remarked 'That must have been a damned good bomb.'

Yet even now one footnote remains to be added, and this on the personal authority of Sir Thomas Sopwith. Once again, Spenser Grey is the dominant figure, though in this instance accompanied by Jerry Aldwell, a Naval engineer officer. The pair, Sir Thomas recalled, were flying the Churchill at Eastchurch when they got into a spin and went into the ground. During take-off, it is believed that they entered a stall at about 50mph, which led to the spin. Thankfully both pilots survived the crash, but the incident helped provide a better understanding of the nature of a spin and avoidance techniques.

Repaired, the aircraft was later used on an abortive attempt to bomb a German airship shed at Cologne. Finally, it was abandoned in Antwerp following the advance of German troops.

The original 1913 Circuit Seaplane.

The Early Circuit Seaplanes

Among the entries for the *Daily Mail* Circuit of Britain race, held from August 16-30, 1913, was a tractor seaplane of the Sopwith Company. The machine was a large four-bay biplane powered by a six-cylinder 100hp Green engine and was flown in the £5,000 contest by Harry Hawker and H Kauper. The Sopwith was the only machine to take-off in the event, the other three entries having withdrawn. The rules of the trial stipulated that the distance of 1,540 miles was to be completed in three days from the start.

The slim, upright engine permitted a clean, tapered nose compared with the blunt front of the landplane version with its 80hp Gnome, but the powerplant gave continual trouble during the race. After two starts, Hawker managed to cover two-thirds of the course, but finally had to give up and was awarded a special personal prize of £1,000 for his determination and display of fine airmanship.

The radiators for the water-cooled Green were mounted on each side of the fuselage, and the centre section of the wings was left uncovered to offer easy egress for the crew in the event of a crash.

That some close association existed between this curious and obscure 'one-off' Sopwith type and the 1914 Circuit Seaplane is apparent from its general appearance, the non-folding wings being the most obvious similarities. To a marked degree, however, the true derivation of the machine is concealed by the unequal-span wings, with strut-braced upper extremities; by the bedazzling effect of the huge roundels painted on the under-surfaces of the upper wings, as well as the lower ones; and most of all, perhaps by the entirely different engine installation.

The engine was, in fact, a water-cooled 120hp Austro-Daimler, the deep frontal radiator for which appears to have been outsize-projecting, as it did, high above the engine itself. The bizarre appearance thus conveyed, was heightened by the echelon arrangement of exhaust ports in the heavily louvered side-cowlings. A long fore-and-aft member lower down and in line with the two cockpits was apparently a foot step. Behind and above the engine was what appears to have been a tank, substantially oblong in form; and on the rearmost inboard bracing strut was a wind-driven pump, or the like. No.137 survived until sometime in 1915, when it was overhauled by Pemberton Billing Ltd.

TECHNICAL DATA 1913 & 1914 CIRCUIT SEAPLANE

ENGINE: (1913) One 100hp Green; (1914) One 100hp Gnome Monosoupape
WING SPAN: (1913) 49ft 6in; (1914) 36ft 6in
LENGTH: (1913) 31ft; (1914 with float landing gear) 30ft 10in
WING AREA: (1913) 500 sq/ft
MAX WEIGHT: (1913) 2,400lb
CRUISING SPEED: (1913) 65 mph

» AUG 16-23, 1913
Daily Mail air race

» 1915
Last record of No.137

Sopwith Type C with Sueter patent torpedo dropping gear pictured at Cowes in early 1914.

» FEB 1914
Admiralty orders special torpedo seaplane

» OCT 1914
Three Type Cs completed

» 1915
Withdrawn from service

A Rare Sopwith Failure

Whether or not Italian pioneering work on aerial torpedo-dropping, dating from 1912, in any way influenced the British Admiralty, has not been positively established. It is, however, recorded that a discussion paper was prepared by Lt D H Hyde-Thomson RN in 1912, setting down suggested parameters for the use of aerial torpedoes; this was submitted to the Admiralty torpedo establishment and eventually reached Capt Murray Fraser Sueter RN of the the Admiralty's Air Department. In 1913, as a direct result of this paper, the Admiralty invited the manufacturers Sopwith, Short and White to produce prototype torpedo-carrying seaplanes. These were to become the Sopwith Special, the Short Type 184 and the Wight Type 840.

Until relatively recently there has been much confusion regarding early Sopwith torpedo-carrying seaplanes, to some extent caused by surviving company records which suggest that all seaplanes ordered by the Admiralty before the First World War and powered by the 200hp Canton-Unne fourteen-cylinder water-cooled radial engine, mounted horizontally, were referred to as Type Cs. There was certainly a Short Type C powered thus, but it was not equipped to carry a torpedo. A surviving Sopwith company photograph was captioned to illustrate a large four-bay seaplane with Canton-Unne engine as a Type C aeroplane. The accuracy of this caption had never been questioned until recent research indicated that the photograph in fact depicts the Sopwith Special, No.170, apparently designed by R J Ashfield, which was an aircraft intended to lift a 14in torpedo weighing 810lbs. Indeed, this was the first British aeroplane designed and built with the specific object of carrying a torpedo.

According to Sqn Cdr Longmore, commanding NAS Calshot, No.170 arrived around July 1, and was assembled within about five days. Engine runs and some taxying trials, however, disclosed that 'extensive' modifications would be needed before the aircraft would succeed in taking off with the torpedo. To begin with, it was found that the engine was not giving full power, and a new engine was fitted, but even when the torpedo was removed the aircraft still refused to take off. Thus, it was to be the Short Type 121 that first took off and launched a torpedo on July 28.

There is no doubt that the Short design was a superior aircraft and, although the Sopwith Special eventually managed at least one flight with pilot (Flt Cdr J L Travers), passenger and a full load of fuel on November 7, it never succeeded in lifting a torpedo. At the end of that month, in a belief that No.170 might be usefully employed as a bomber, the seaplane was fitted with an experimental bomb rack, but it is not known whether it was ever flown in this configuration. In April 1915, the Special was removed from RNAS charge and during the following weeks it was dismantled.

Unfortunately very little information of a reliable nature survives about the Sopwith Type C, other than reference to three such aircraft, Nos.157-159, in the RNAS equipment lists; these seaplanes (and the six Short Type Cs, Nos.161-166) were categorised as 'bomb-carriers' with folding wings, wireless equipment and a defensive gun. However, there is no evidence that the Sopwith Type Cs ever flew with a bomb load and, as they do not appear to have undergone trials with the RNAS at Calshot, there are no surviving records of flight trials.

TECHNICAL DATA TYPE C

ENGINE: One 205hp Canton-Unne (Salmson)

WING SPAN: (Upper) 66ft; (Lower) 58ft

LENGTH: 36ft

WING AREA: 785 sq/ft

MAX ALL-UP WEIGHT: 4,324lb

Howard Pixton (leaning against leading edge of the wing) in relaxed mood, during the Schneider Trophy competition in Monaco in 1914.

Record-Breaking Seaplane

>> **NOV 27, 1913**
Maiden flight by Harry Hawker

>> **APR 20, 1914**
Aircraft wins Schneider Trophy in Monaco

>> **NOV 1914**
Production begins

The Schneider was so named because it was directly descended from the Sopwith Tabloid seaplane which had been used by Howard Pixton to win the Schneider Trophy contest for Great Britain at Monaco on April 20, 1914. The little Tabloid performed magnificently; its average speed was over 86 mph, and in an extra two laps after finishing the race Pixton reached 92 mph, which was then a world record for seaplanes.

It was natural that with the outbreak of war the RNAS should adopt this fine seaplane, and production began in November 1914 with an order for twelve aircraft, Nos.1436 to 1447. The early RNAS Schneiders differed little from Pixton's Tabloid. The same 100hp Monosoupape Gnome engine was used, housed in a curious bull-nosed cowling which became a characteristic feature of the Schneider and in fact distinguished the type from the later Baby. Early aircraft had a triangular fin and employed wing-warping; later an enlarged, curved fin and normal ailerons were introduced, as in the three-view drawing. Subsequent orders were for 24 Schneiders (Nos.1556 to 1579) followed by another 100 (Nos.3707 to 3806), and the final production total was 160, five of which remained in commission in March 1918.

During 1915 repeated attempts were made to use Schneiders to intercept Zeppelins over the North Sea. The seaplanes were carried aboard light cruisers, paddle-steamers such as *Killingholme* and *Brocklesby*, and in the seaplane-carriers *Ben-my-Chree* and *Engadine*. Scant success attended these sorties; frequently the seaplanes could not take off due to heavy seas, or the floats broke up in the water. A remedy was sought by fitting two-wheeled dollies beneath the floats, enabling the Schneiders to operate from the short flying-off deck of carriers so equipped. The first successful take-off using this device was from *Campania* on August 6, 1915 with Flt Lt W L Welsh flying the Schneider.

Overseas, Schneiders did an immense amount of useful work, both reconnaissance and fighting, in the eastern Mediterranean and the Red Sea. They saw service in the Dardanelles campaign, flying from *Ark Royal*, and as late as November 21, 1916 a Schneider, flown by Flt Sub Lt A F Brandon, shot down an enemy aircraft over Mudros.

TECHNICAL DATA - SCHNEIDER

ENGINE: One 100hp Gnome Monosoupape	**LOADED WEIGHT:** 1,700lb
WING SPAN: 25ft 8in	**MAX SPEED:** 87 mph
LENGTH: 22ft 10in	**SERVICE CEILING:** 8,000ft
HEIGHT: 10ft	**CLIMB RATE:** 6,500ft in 15mins
WING AREA: 240 sq/ft	**ARMAMENT:** One .303in Lewis machine gun and one 65lb bomb
EMPTY WEIGHT: 1,220lb	

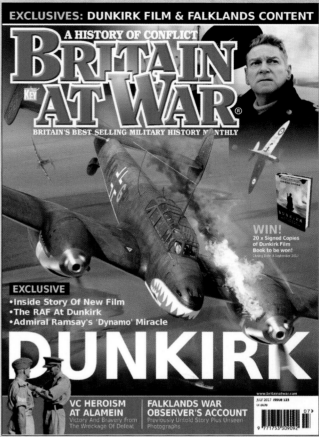

Sopwith Gunbus (Admiralty Type 806), with bomb-carriers outboard of the revised undercarriage and two-wheel landing gear, used a Sunbeam engine. Many were built by Robey & Co. of Lincoln.

» OCT 25, 1913
Contract issued by Admiralty

» JUL-OCT 1914
No.897-901 delivered to the Admiralty

TECHNICAL DATA GUNBUS

ENGINE: One 150hp Sunbeam Crusader

WING SPAN: 50ft

LENGTH: 32ft 6in

HEIGHT: 11ft 4in

WING AREA: 474 sq/ft

MAX SPEED: 80 mph

SERVICE CEILING: 5,000ft

CLIMB RATE: 3,500ft in 15mins

ENDURANCE: 2½hrs

ARMAMENT: One .303in Lewis machine gun and provision for bombs

Single-engined pusher biplane

The Gunbus was essentially a landplane derivative of the SPGn (Sopwith Pusher, gun), a gun-carrying two-seat pusher biplane with twin floats. Six of these floatplanes were ordered from the recently-founded Sopwith Aviation Company by the Greek government in March 1914, but were immediately commandeered by the Admiralty when war was declared in August that year, subsequently serving with the RNAS. The Gunbus, intended for the fighting role, carried a 0.303in machine gun on a flexible mount in the forward cockpit and was powered by a 100hp Gnome Monosoupape rotary engine. A more powerful version, with a 150hp Sunbeam eight-cylinder water-cooled engine, was developed specifically for the RNAS, this having a redesigned nacelle and a revised undercarriage. Six of the Sunbeam-powered Gunbuses were built for the RNAS by Sopwith, a further 30 being ordered for the service from Robey & Company, these last being intended for bombing (and possibly anti-submarine) duties as distinct from fighting. The pilot was moved forward to the front cockpit, a bombing panel being set into the floor and four bomb carriers being fitted beneath the lower wing. The following data relates to the Sunbeam-powered two-seat fighter Gunbus.

The 150hp Sunbeam was a fairly obscure powerplant, and one with particular RNAS associations. Like the Rolls-Royce Hawk, it seemingly achieved its greatest distinction in airships. Perhaps the most noticeable feature of the Admiralty Type 806 was its new two-wheel cross-axle landing gear, with revised attachments and bracing. Though the track of this new gear - the wheels of which were rubber-bound and

attached to skids - was relatively narrow, this was greatly accentuated by the 50ft wing span.

What may be considered as the definitive version of the Gunbus (for, as noted at the outset, production was still in hand late into 1915) was not built by Sopwith, but by Robey & Co Ltd of Lincoln. That the order called for only thirty machines, and had been placed (in May 1915) with an engineering company that dated far back into Victorian times, may at first seem strange. However, the order could be compared with at least two other obscure contracts for pushers-specifically the DH.1As from Savages Ltd. of Kings Lynn, Norfolk, and the Vickers FB.9s from Wells Aviation Co Ltd. of Chelsea, London (the latter, for some mysterious reason, having different 'wire' lengths from FB.9s built by Vickers themselves). A second point is that the Robey-built Sopwith Gunbuses had tangible Sopwith associations: Harry Hawker himself tested the first machine of the batch - No.3833 (the total order was 3833-3862, from 3850 onwards being delivered as spares); the first two examples at least were sent to Brooklands; and the drawings used by Robey were the responsibility of Sopwith's 'super draughtsman' R J Ashfield.

Whatever name or designation they may have gone by, it seems tolerably certain that the Robey-built Gunbuses were constructed with bombing in mind: for not only was the pilot moved to the front cockpit in the lengthened nacelle, but there were underwing carriers (set close inboard) for four - and latterly, with reduced petrol capacity - six - 65lbs bombs.

Hardly surprisingly, some of these pushers did serve as trainers - at Hendon and at Eastchurch.

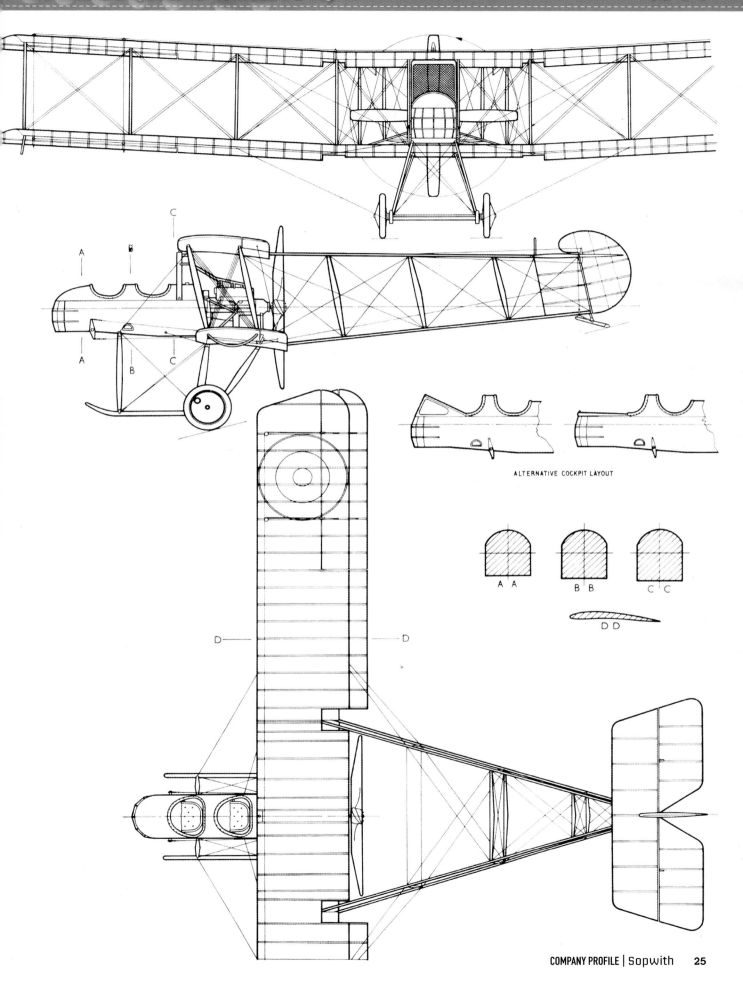

ALTERNATIVE COCKPIT LAYOUT

A A   B B   C C

D D

The Type 807 was based on the earlier 'Round Britain' contest seaplane.

Circuit of Britain Machine Destined for War

>> **AUG 29, 1914**
First of three batches ordered by the Admiralty

>> **MAR 1915**
Last deliveries to the RNAS

>> **1916**
No.920 still in use as a landplane

The Sopwith entry in the 1914 *Daily Mail* Circuit of Britain contest consisted of a two-seat biplane which was an enlarged Tabloid in general appearance. It was allotted race number '1', with Victor Mahl chosen as the pilot.

The two-bay wings were of equal span and were staggered, with ailerons of inverse taper fitted to all four tips. The view from the pilot's rear cockpit was assisted by the 12in stagger and cut-outs in both upper centre-section and lower wing-roots. The Circuit entry was flown first at Brooklands as a landplane before the installation of the stepless floats. These were spaced well apart and were pivoted at the front, leaf springs providing shock-absorbing at the rear. At the same time the fin and rudder area was increased to balance the addition of forward side area.

While the Circuit seaplane was being prepared, a production batch was being built for the Navy, and this version became known as the Admiralty Type 807 from the serial number of the first machine constructed. The same 100hp Monosoupape Gnome engine was used in the production 807s, but the Admiralty seaplane differed in several

respects. The Short patent wing-folding device was incorporated, and the wings were without stagger to simplify the operation. The upper wings were increased in span and the extensions were braced by wires and king-posts. The lower wings were shortened slightly, and the pilot occupied the rear seat, with his observer in the front cockpit. Delivery of the 807 to the Admiralty was made in July, 1914, just before the start of hostilities. Twelve, at least, are believed to have entered service, to be used subsequently with the RNAS at Calshot, Great Yarmouth, the Dardanelles, in East Africa and aboard the seaplane-carrier HMS *Ark Royal*.

TECHNICAL DATA - TYPE 807

ENGINE: One 100hp Gnome Monosoupape

WING SPAN: (Upper) 43ft 6in; (Lower) 33ft

LENGTH: 30ft 9in

WING AREA: 405 sq/ft

EMPTY WEIGHT: 1,580lb

ALL-UP WEIGHT: 2,440lb

MAX SPEED: 80 mph

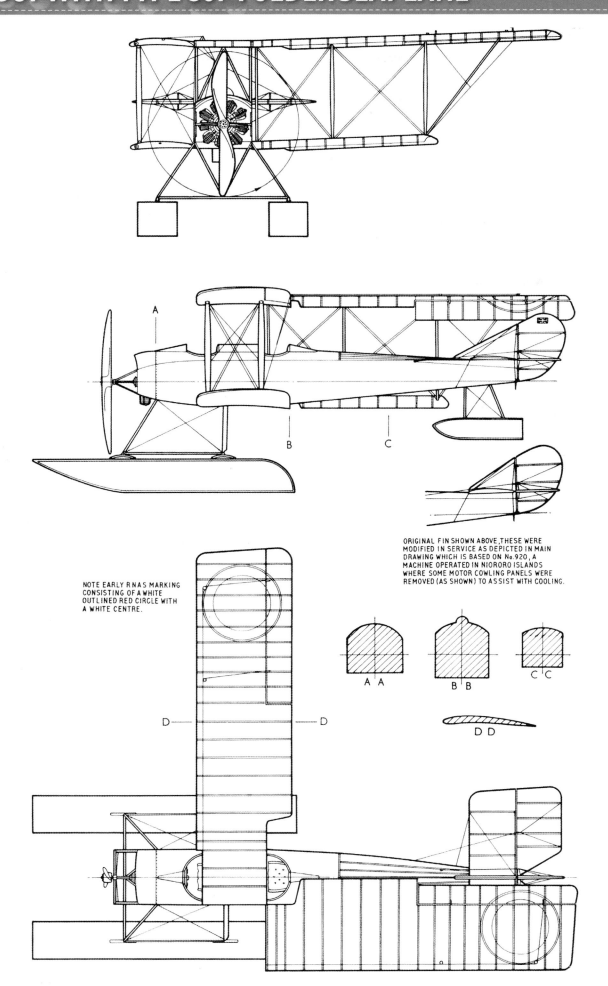

ORIGINAL FIN SHOWN ABOVE, THESE WERE
MODIFIED IN SERVICE AS DEPICTED IN MAIN
DRAWING WHICH IS BASED ON No. 920, A
MACHINE OPERATED IN NIORORO ISLANDS
WHERE SOME MOTOR COWLING PANELS WERE
REMOVED (AS SHOWN) TO ASSIST WITH COOLING.

NOTE EARLY RNAS MARKING
CONSISTING OF A WHITE
OUTLINED RED CIRCLE WITH
A WHITE CENTRE.

A A

B B

C C

D D

Sopwith Type 860 Seaplane, No.859 during trials on the Isle of Grain in 1916.

TECHNICAL DATA TYPE 860 SEAPLANE

ENGINE: One 225hp Sunbeam Mohawk or one 200hp Salmson 2M7

WING SPAN: 62ft 11in

WING AREA: 790 sq/ft

ARMAMENT: Possibly one .303in Lewis machine gun and one 810lb 14in Whitehead torpedo

>> **DEC 1914**

Maiden flight of the Type 860

>> **JAN 27, 1915**

First flight with a torpedo

>> **1916**

Withdrawn from home water patrols

In the Shadow of the Type 184

Experience with the early torpedo-carrying seaplanes had demonstrated to two of the three main Admiralty contractors that the smaller Salmson and Sunbeam engines were inadequate to enable torpedo-carriers to lift off the water when carrying a full fuel load. After the unsuccessful attempts by the Sopwith Special No.170 to lift a torpedo into the air in August 1914, it was decided to produce a smaller aircraft, powered by the 225hp Sunbeam (later named the Mohawk). In the meantime Sopwith persevered with another of its seaplanes, No.138, powered by a 200hp Canton Unne engine and on August 29, 1914, flown by Longmore, this machine succeeded in lifting and launching an 810lb torpedo at Calshot.

Continuing frustration with the Canton Unne engine encouraged Sopwith to adopt the 225hp Sunbeam, at the time the most powerful engine available to the RNAS. No prototype of the new aircraft was built and a total of 22 examples ordered during the autumn of 1914. All but four were completed between December that year and early in 1915. The first ten examples were numbered 851-860, and were referred to as Admiralty Type 860s (although confusion was compounded when the RNAS equipment list erroneously referred to them as Type 157s, suggesting that they were a production batch of Sopwith Type Cs). The first flight by a Type 860 with a torpedo was made by Sopwith pilot Victor Mahl at Calshot on January 27, 1915.

The big Sunbeam engine, driving either a two- or four-blade propeller, featured a frontal radiator and a prominent stack of twelve vertical exhaust pipes extending upwards immediately forward of the upper wing. Long struts to the lower fuselage longerons attached the single-step main pontoon floats with the 14in torpedo being carried on crutches at the centre of the crossbars between the

floats. When the aircraft was at rest on the water, the torpedo was partly submerged. A single tail float was provided, as well as stabilizing wingtip floats.

Folding wings of at least three alternative designs appeared on production aircraft; the original three-bay wings of equal span were fitted with double-acting ailerons on both upper and lower surfaces. Some aircraft were fitted with two-bay wings of unequal span with ailerons on the upper wing only; the outboard upper wing extensions were wire-braced with kingposts, but some aircraft featured outwardly raked struts in place of interplane wire bracing. At an early stage in production the fin, originally a small triangular structure, was enlarged to incorporate a curved leading edge. Further redesign resulted in a rectangular fin being fitted.

The Sopwith Type 860 was flown from the rear cockpit, a surprising decision bearing in mind its torpedo-dropping role. The observer's cockpit was located beneath a large aperture in the upper wing centre-section, suggesting that it was intended to mount an upward firing Lewis gun, though no evidence has been found to suggest that this was ever fitted, despite being called for in the original Admiralty purchase order.

Production Type 860s are said to have been test flown from the Solent and subsequently served briefly with the RNAS at Grain, though without much distinction. The greater experience gained by Short Brothers in numerous aspects of naval seaplane design inclined the Admiralty to favour that company's parallel project, the Type 184, which was to become one of the outstanding British seaplane bombers of the First World War. Certainly the Sopwith aircraft never launched a torpedo in anger.

Officially known as the Two-seater Scout, this aeroplane was more or less a landplane version of the Type 807 and at least 24 were delivered to the RNAS, being employed on anti-Zeppelin patrols from Hendon, Great Yarmouth and Killingholme. *IWM*

Sopwith's 'Spinning Jenny'

'Spinning Jenny' was the name by which this generally unpopular biplane became known to its RNAS crews - a name which first came prominently to public attention (as, indeed, did the aeroplane itself) during the 1950s by reason of recollections then aired by Sqn Ldr J C Brooke, RAF (Ret).

While based at Killingholme, this former RNAS officer had experienced the propensity of this particular Sopwith aeroplane to spin at the least provocation. From his first unpremeditated spin on the type (No.1055 was the machine concerned) he regained control, and next day did two deliberate spins, though recovering from both only after a loss of 1,000ft.

That the Sopwith 1914 Circuit Seaplane had been built to drawings marked 'D3' has already been recorded. However, it was also evident that the Folder Seaplane and the Two-seat Scout (which appeared in March 1915, a few months after the Folder), shared common ground - widely spaced cockpits with headrest fairings and a low-powered rotary engine being earmarks of the breed. Apart from the obvious distinctions in landing gear, and non-folding wings of equal span (36ft 11in) the Two-seater Scout had a shorter fuselage (apparently omitting one bay) which could well be accounted for by its smaller side area, as compared with the Folder Seaplane, with its floats. Strut-connected ailerons were fitted on all four wings, and the tail resembled that of the Folder. The main landing gear was of simple V-strut form (made taller when bombs were carried, as later described), and though the tailskid was sturdy and tall, the overall appearance of the Two-seater Scout was considered trim, and worthy, perhaps, of a more powerful engine (the spinning tendency notwithstanding). Weight is

lent to this reasoning as the type is known to have gone to war not only with assorted small arms (though not machine-guns), - and bombs, carried either additionally or as an alternative load.

It is important here to note that during 1915 bombs were regarded as anti-airship, as well as air-to-ground weapons; and thus the Sopwith Two-seater Scouts that were based not only at Killingholme, but at Hendon, Chingford and Great Yarmouth also, may indeed have been fulfilling the contemporary function of 'scout' - in the sense that their purpose was air fighting rather than reconnaissance, or 'scouting' in the earlier tradition.

In general form - and especially in being strut-attached far below the fuselage - the bomb installation resembled that found on some Sopwith Schneiders. The bombs themselves, which were to some extent between the rear legs of the heightened landing gear, could well have been of the pattern called 'small petrol bomb', the 16lb carcass incendiary, the 16lb H.E.R.L. or the 20lb Hales HE. The familiar '20lb Cooper' had not at that time arrived, although an early form of Cooper fuse was designed for anti-aircraft work, and its designer had early associations with F Marten Hale. Should a bombsight of any kind have been fitted this might well have been of the 'Lever' type, then used by the RNAS.

The last of twenty-four Sopwith Two-seater Scouts (Nos. 1051-1074) were delivered to RNAS Chingford in June 1915. At the time, W R D Shaw, of Chingford Road, Walthamstow, was linked with a scheme for fitting an aeroplane, generally resembling the Two-seater Scout, with a tailplane having 'a negative dihedral angle to prevent a spin or nosedive due to side-slip when banking'.

>> **NOV 1914**
Maiden flight

>> **JUN 1915**
Final example delivered to Chingford

TECHNICAL DATA SPINNING JENNY
ENGINE: One 100hp Gnome Monosoupape
WING SPAN: 36ft 6in
LENGTH: 30ft 9½in
HEIGHT: 10ft
EMPTY WEIGHT: 1,210lb
ALL-UP WEIGHT: 1,950lb
MAX SPEED: 69 mph
SERVICE CEILING: 3,000ft
ARMAMENT: Rudimentary combination of grenades, pistols or rifles

Two examples of these single-seat tractor biplanes were constructed during 1914 for the Gordon Bennett Race of that year, and were improved versions of the Tabloid featuring circular fuselages.

TECHNICAL DATA GORDON BENNETT RACER

ENGINE: One 80hp Gnome
MAX SPEED: 105 mph

>> **OCT 19, 1914**
No.1214 delivered to Hendon

>> **JUL 1915**
No.1215 withdrawn at Chingford

>> **MAR 1916**
No.1214 withdrawn

A Racer in the Hands of the Military

The 'Gordon Bennet' racer was interestingly described in a contemporary report from the time, as follows: 'The first of these machines, was very distinctive, not only in matters of detail wherein it differed from any known form of the Tabloid, but in palpably basic features also. That this particular aeroplane had a special claim to the name 'Gordon Bennett' or 'Gordon Bennett Racer'; that it was taken over by the Admiralty as No.1215; and that it had associations, at Hendon, with Lt Spenser Grey are indisputable facts; but concerning the second aeroplane mentioned some haziness persists, though in having tucked it away under the 'Tabloid' heading one feels relief and confidence in equal measure. Let us then recognise what the above photograph proclaims it to be a Tabloid, or a very close derivative. But equally let us admit the possibility of its having been intended (in one form or another) as a standby, or second siring, for the 1914 Gordon Bennett Aviation Cup.'

On the purely sporting aspects of the matter , we turn to Peter Lewis, writing in 1914. Thus: 'Racing had been extremely popular for some three years, but relatively few attempts had been made in Great Britain to design small machines exclusively for the purpose. Among the efforts just before the war began was the Sopwith single-seater derived from the Tabloid with the express intention of competing for the 1914 Gordon Bennett Aviation Cup. It used an 80hp Gnome equipped with a deep-chord cowling blended into a finely conceived circular fuselage but was never raced and, instead, saw war service at Hendon in the RNAS as 1215.'

He continues: 'The most noticeable differences between the special Gordon Bennett machine and a typical Tabloid were the slender fuselage, with convex side-fairings running back to the deep-chord tailplane, and blending forwards with a particularly smooth cowling having an annular air-intake of very small diameter, behind the propeller spinner; the vertical tail-surfaces alarmingly small in area, even though disposed both above and below the fuselage (the triangular fins seeming almost negligible ahead of the deep-chord, shallow and rounded rudder); and the slimness of the V-form landing gear struts.

'Yet there were distinctions also in the wing cellule which, though generally of Tabloid form, had no stagger, and was braced by notably slender steel-tube struts, those immediately forward of the cockpit converging sharply upwards in side elevation, though the rear struts were single, and not inverted-Vs as on the 1915 Martinsyde two-seater, which had a somewhat similar arrangement. Behind the cockpit was the merest suggestion of a head-fairing, and another probably more significant subtlety was the blending of the lower wing-roots with the rounded fuselage, somewhat as on the Gloster IV racing seaplane of 1927.

'It appeared, indeed, that the only discernible feature having some possible commonality between Gordon Bennett No.1215 and Tabloid (or Tabloid-derivative) No.1214 was the low-drag landing gear; and that 1215 should be appreciably the faster of the pair having a reputed speed of 105 mph with a Gnome engine of only 80hp can well be understood.

'Less comprehensible, having regard to the fact that the 1913 Gordon Bennett contest had been won, by a Deperdussin monoplane, at 124 mph, is that any hope whatever should have been entertained for competitive success, though a more powerful engine may well have been in view.'

Early in 1914 the Tabloid was put into production as a single-seat scout for both the Military and Naval Wings of the RFC

Schneider Winner turned Military Scout

The Tabloid was one of the most outstanding aircraft produced in Great Britain before the outbreak of war in 1914. By the standards of those days, its top speed of over 90 mph and its climb of 1,200 ft/min placed it in a class of its own, and it caused a sensation when demonstrated in public for the first time by Harry Hawker, at Hendon on November 29,1913. The prototype seated two, side-by-side, but subsequent Tabloids were single-seaters, including the seaplane flown to victory in the 1914 Schneider Trophy contest by Howard Pixton,

The military potential of the Tabloid was immediately apparent and production for the Naval and Military Wings of the RFC began early in 1914. By October 1914 the RNAS possessed only three Tabloids,

yet in that month the type struck a telling blow against the enemy. On October 8, Sqn Cdr Spenser Grey and Flt Lt R L G Marix took off from Antwerp, then under bombardment by the enemy, in Tabloids Nos.167 and 168 to bomb the Zeppelin sheds at Cologne and Düsseldorf. Mist prevented Spenser Grey from finding his target, so he bombed Cologne railway station, but Marix's success was complete. He dived on the sheds at Düsseldorf and bombed from 600ft. Within 30 seconds flames had risen to 500ft; the new Zeppelin IX had been destroyed, the first to fall victim to a British aircraft.

Between October 1914 and June 1915, a further 36 Tabloids were built and delivered to the RFC and RNAS. The naval Tabloids served with Wg Cdr Samson's Eastchurch squadron in Belgium, as already mentioned, and later with Samson's 3 Squadron, RNAS, in the Dardanelles campaign. Others served aboard the seaplane-carrier *Ark Royal* in the same campaign, and at least one Tabloid was on the strength of the RNAS station at Great Yarmouth.

A Tabloid, although the serial (A394) indicates a Baby, in US Navy hands complete with a four-blade propeller and the original fin.

TECHNICAL DATA - TABLOID

ENGINE: One 100hp Gnome Monosoupape	**MAX SPEED:** 93 mph at sea level
WING SPAN: 25ft 6in	**CLIMB RATE:** 1,200ft in 1min
LENGTH: 20ft 4in	
HEIGHT: 8ft 5in	**ENDURANCE:** 3½hrs
WING AREA: 241 sq/ft	**ARMAMENT:** One.303in Lewis machine gun and a small load of 20lb bombs
EMPTY WEIGHT: 730lb	
LOADED WEIGHT: 1,120lb	

» NOV 29, 1913
First public appearance

» NOV 1913
Military place order for a dozen aircraft

» SEP 22, 1914
Tabloids carry out first raid on German soil

» OCT 8, 1914
Two Tabloids attack Zeppelin sheds in Antwerp

» JAN 1915
Tabloid withdrawn from RFC service

» FEB 1915
Samson's squadron mount Lewis guns above upper wing

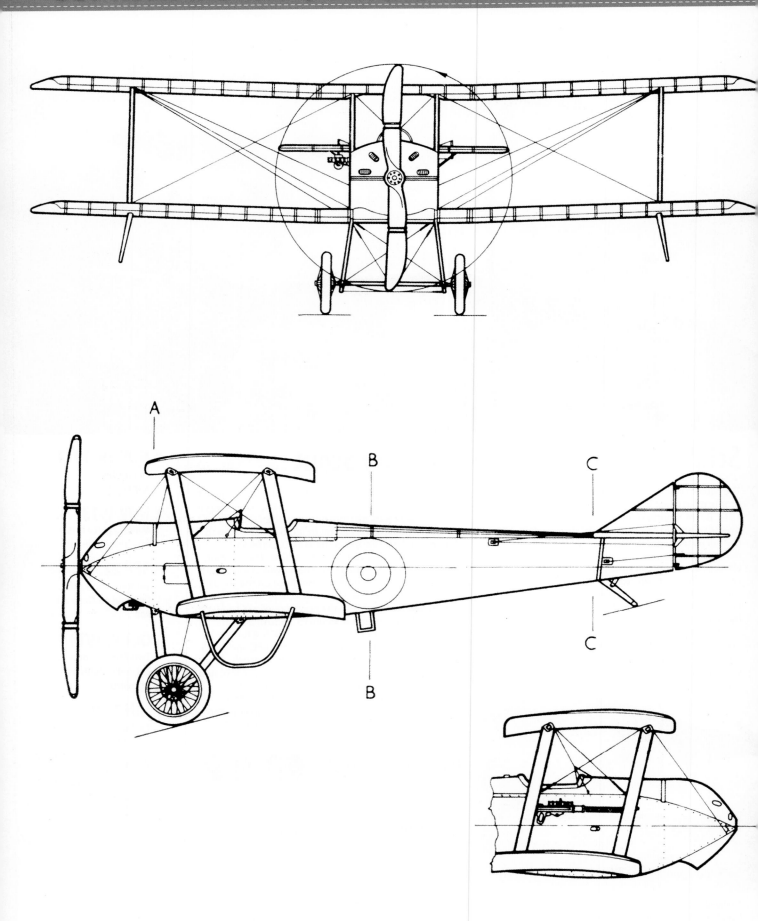

A

B

C

C

B

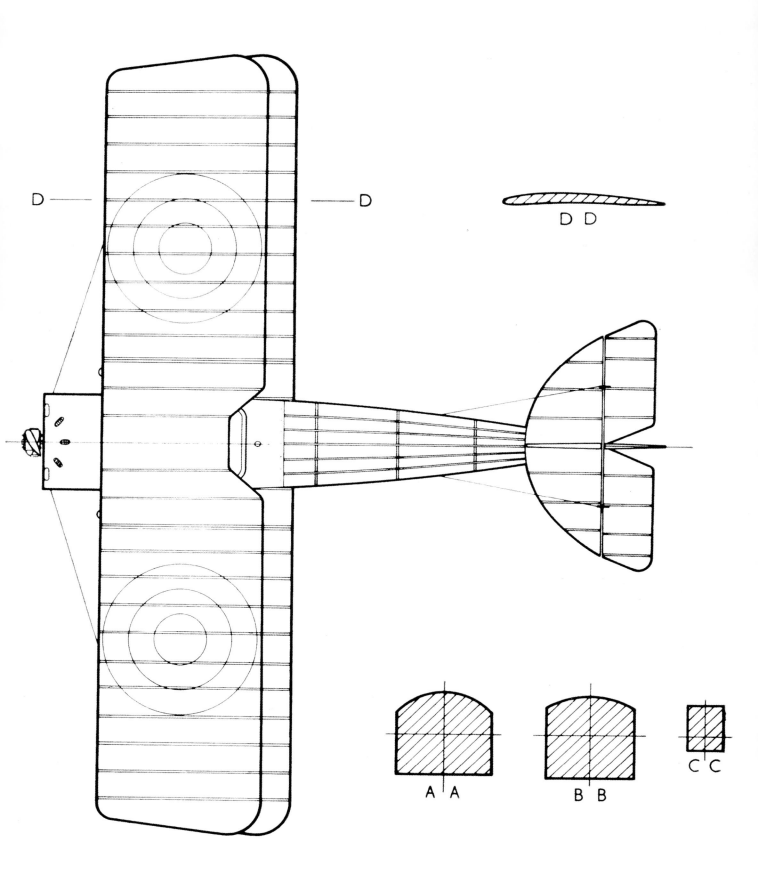

D ———— D

D D

A A

B B

C C

Derived from the Schneider single-seat fighter seaplane, the Baby first appeared in September 1915, and differed from its predecessor primarily in having a 110hp Clerget nine-cylinder rotary in place of the Monosoupape, this being accommodated by a horseshoe-shaped open-fronted cowling.

≫ SEP 1915
Maiden flight and first production deliveries

≫ JUL 1916
Last of first batch of 100 aircraft delivered

≫ DEC 1916
***Ben-my-Chree* Babies bomb Chikaldir Bridge**

≫ JAN 20, 1918
Two Babies try to bomb German cruiser *Goeben*

≫ 1923
Type retired by Chilean and Italian Navys

≫ 1931
Norwegian Air Force Babies finally retired

A Very Feisty and Purposeful Infant

The Sopwith Baby was a development of the Schneider, from which it differed in having the more powerful 110hp Clerget engine in place of the Gnome Monosoupape and the bull-nosed cowling of the earlier aircraft replaced by an open-fronted cowling of more orthodox pattern. Another improvement was the installation of a synchronised Lewis gun above the fuselage, though some Babies retained the original type of gun-mounting with the Lewis inclined upwards through the top wing. The first batch of 100 Babies (Nos.8118 to 8217) were built by Sopwith and delivered between September 1915 and July 1916. The first five aircraft of this batch retained the 100hp Gnome engine, as did No. 8199. The rest had the 110hp Clerget, and this engine was retained when Baby production was transferred to the Blackburn Company.

The first Blackburn Baby (N300) was followed by 70 production aircraft with 110hp Clerget engines (N1010 to N1039, N1060 to N1069 and N1100 to N1129) and 115 with the 130hp Clerget powerplant (N1410 to N1449 and N2060 to N2134). It had originally been planned to fit the Bentley AR.1 from N1410, but these engines were not available in time. The first batch of 130hp Babies differed from the others in having Ranken anti-Zeppelin darts fitted instead of a machine-gun.

In the same way as the Schneiders, Babies operated from seaplane-carriers in the North Sea and the Mediterranean. They also flew on fighter patrols from Dunkirk until superseded by Sopwith Pups in July 1917. In the various Middle East campaigns, Babies were frequently used in bombing raids. *Ben-my-Chree's* Babies attacked the Chikaldir railway bridge in December 1916, and, in November, those from the

carrier *Empress* took part in the Palestine fighting. Bombing raids on Zeppelin bases from home waters were less successful. In an attack on the Tondern airship base from the carriers *Engadine* and *Vindex* on May 4, 1916 only one out of eleven Babies succeeded in bombing the target.

One Baby seaplane (N2078) survives and is on exhibition at the FAA Museum at Yeovilton.

Units

The type was used by RNAS coastal air stations at Calshot, Dundee, Dunkirk, Felixstowe, Fishguard, Great Yarmouth, Killingholme, Scapa Flow and Westgate.

Overseas units were based at Alexandria, Otranto, Port Said, Santa Maria di Leuca, Souda bay and Thasos.

The Baby also flew from the seaplane carriers *Ben-my-Chree, Campania, City of Oxford, Empress, Engadine, Furious, Manxman, Peony, Raven II, Riviera* and *Vindex*.

TECHNICAL DATA - BABY

ENGINE: One 110hp or 130hp Clerget	**MAX SPEED:** 100 mph at sea level
WING SPAN: 25ft 8in	**CLIMB RATE:** 10,000ft in 35min
LENGTH: 23ft	
HEIGHT: 10ft	**ENDURANCE:** 2¼hrs
WING AREA: 240 sq/ft	**ARMAMENT:** One .303in Lewis machine gun and provision for a pair of 65lb bombs
EMPTY WEIGHT: 1,226lb	
LOADED WEIGHT: 1,715lb	

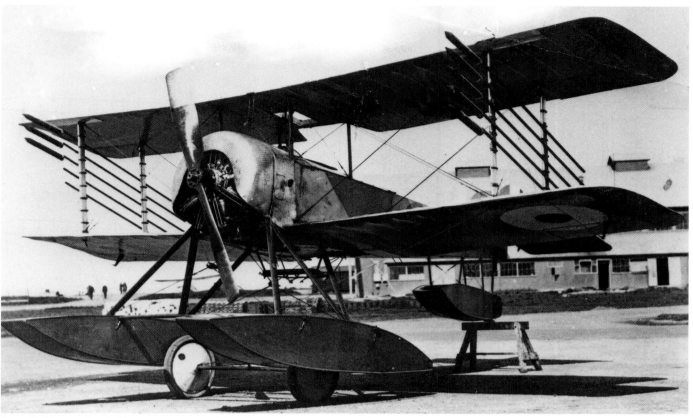

Several Babies were fitted with two 0.303in guns side by side over the wing; one batch of Blackburn-built Babies was fitted with Ranken explosive darts as anti-airship weapons, and at least one was fitted with Le Prieur rockets, 10 of these devices being attached to the interplane bracing struts.

The sole surviving example of a Sopwith Baby Seaplane after the completion of its restoration/re-build at Fleetlands in 1970. The aircraft can be seen at FAA Museum at Yeovilton.

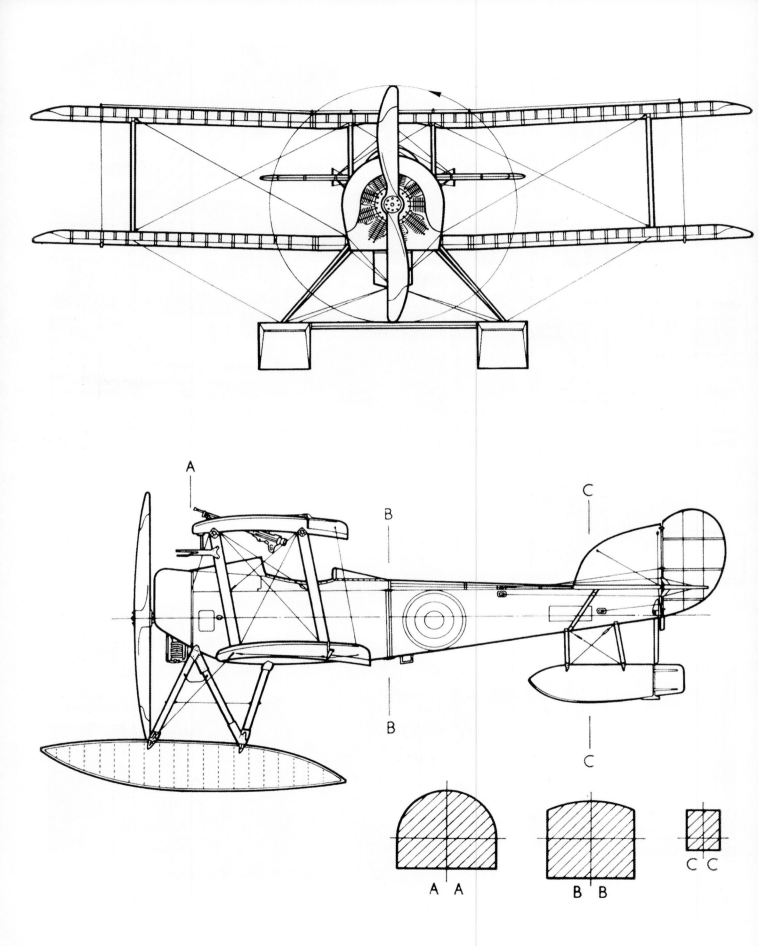

A

B

C

C

B

A A

B B

C C

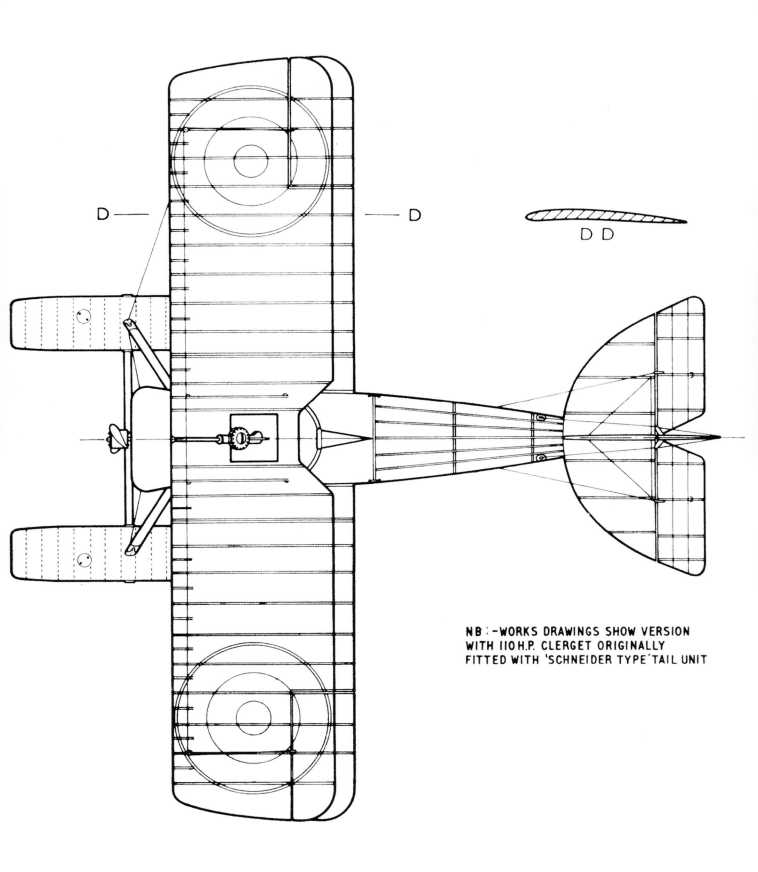

D — — D

D D

NB :-WORKS DRAWINGS SHOW VERSION
WITH 110 H.P. CLERGET ORIGINALLY
FITTED WITH 'SCHNEIDER TYPE' TAIL UNIT

SOPWITH 1 ½ STRUTTER

Design of the Sopwith 1½ Strutter probably began quite early in 1915 although, being in effect a private venture at the outset, manufacture of a prototype at Kingston was accorded less urgency than to aeroplanes being prepared to specific Admiralty orders.

» **DEC 1915**
Maiden flight of the prototype

» **FEB 1916**
First deliveries to the RNAS

» **APR 1916**
Enters service with 5 Wing, RNAS

» **JAN 1917**
Obsolete as a fighter

» **SEP 17, 1917**
Possible U-boat sunk by a 65lb bomb

» **1924**
Type withdrawn by the Mexican Air Force

Britain's First Fighter with a Synchronised Gun

Best-known as the Sopwith 1½ Strutter, a name derived from the arrangement of the interplane struts of this single-seat bomber/two-seat fighter biplane, this aircraft had the official Admiralty and RFC designations of Sopwith Type 9700 and Sopwith Two-Seater respectively. The two-seat prototype, flown in late 1915 on the power of a 110hp Clerget rotary engine, introduced air brakes and a variable-incidence tailplane, and when production examples entered service with the RNAS in early 1916 it was the first British aircraft to be equipped with synchronising gear to allow the forward machine-gun to fire through the propeller arc. Both single and two-seat versions were built with 110hp and 130hp Clerget rotaries, but some two-seaters were also powered by the 110hp Le Rhône rotary engine.

When first introduced into service on the Western Front the 1½ Strutter had the edge in combat with German fighters, but it was surpassed in performance within a few months by the Albatros and Halberstadt scouts introduced by the enemy. However, RNAS 1½ Strutters had a longer operational life and towards the end of the war were in service as ship-based aircraft with both skids or conventional wheeled undercarriage. On April 4, 1918 one took-off from a platform mounted over a gun turret of HMAS *Australia*, the first two-seat aircraft to take off from a British warship.

A total of some 1,513 Sopwith 1 1/2 Strutters are believed to have been built for the RFC and RNAS, and the type was also produced in France to a total of two or three times this number. In addition to their use by British forces, this remarkable little aeroplane saw service in and/or after the First World War with the air arms of Belgium, France, Japan, Latvia, Romania, Russia and the American Expeditionary Force.

Units Allocated

Nos. 2, 4, 5, 7 and 8 Squadrons, RNAS (Western Front); Macedonian units: 'A' Squadron (Thasos), 'B' Squadron (later 23 (Naval)) (Mitylene), 'C' Squadron (later 20 (Naval)) (Imbros and Mudros), 'D' Squadron (Stavros), 'E' Squadron (Hadzi Junas) and 'F' Squadron (Amberkoj). RNAS coastal air stations at Dover, Great Yarmouth, Mullion, Otranto, Pembroke and Prawle Point. RNAS training schools at Cranwell and Manston. Aircraft-carriers: *Argus*, *Furious* and *Vindex*. Battleships: *Australia*, *Barham*, *Queen Elizabeth* and *Repulse*.

TECHNICAL DATA - 1½ STRUTTER

ENGINE: One 130hp Clerget 9B

WING SPAN: 33ft 6in

LENGTH: 25ft 3in

HEIGHT: 10ft 3in

WING AREA: 346 sq/ft

EMPTY WEIGHT: 1,305lb

LOADED WEIGHT: 2,149lb

MAX SPEED: 100 mph at 6,500ft

CLIMB RATE: 6,500ft in 9min 10sec

SERVICE CEILING: 15,500ft

ENDURANCE: 3¾hrs

ARMAMENT: One forward-firing .303in Vickers machine-gun and .303in Lewis in rear cockpit and up to 130lb of bombs

Structurally the 1½ Strutter was entirely conventional by Sopwith standards, that is to say it was of all-wood construction with ply and fabric covering; ailerons were fitted to upper and lower wings, which were of equal span. Early aircraft were fitted with the 110hp Clerget engine, but also came to be powered by the 130 and 135hp Clergets and Le Rhône engines of similar power.

Right: A Sopwith 1½ Strutter leaving the gun-turret platform of HMS *Barham*.

Below: Sopwith 1½ Strutter equipped with a pair of upward or forward firing .303in Lewis machine guns.

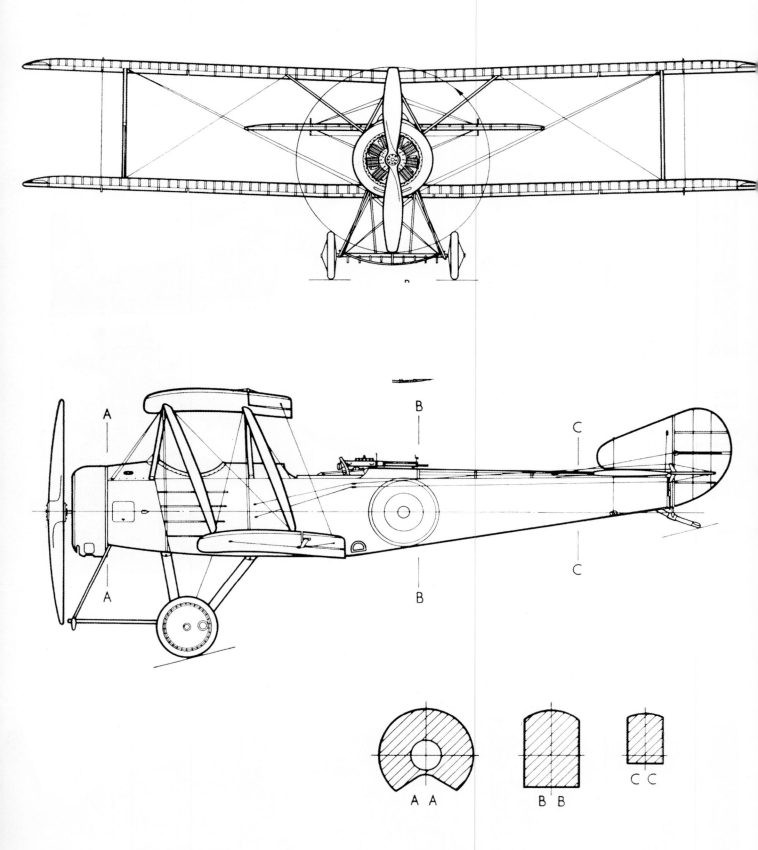

A A   B B   C C

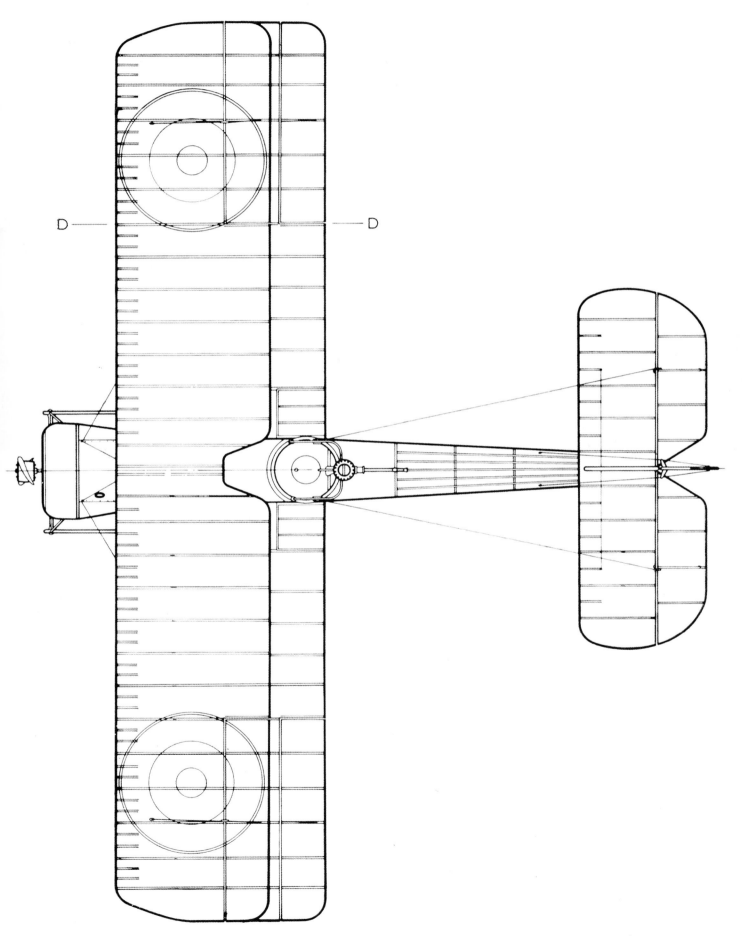

SOPWITH SCOUT (PUP)

RNAS Sopwith Pup, N5180 at Brooklands.

The perfect flying machine

An elegant little equal-span biplane, the Sopwith Admiralty Type 9901 retained the same form of interplane struts adopted for the 1½ Strutter, but with 20% less span, it is not surprising that it became regarded as a 'pup' of the earlier aircraft. The nickname Pup, given by air and ground crews, has long outlived the official designation and the name Sopwith Pup is well endorsed in British aviation history. As first flown this single-seat fighter was powered by an 80hp Le Rhône rotary engine, and the fact that with this low-powered unit it was a highly manoeuvrable and effective fighter speaks volumes for its design and construction. The Pup entered service with both the RAF and RNAS in 1916, and its reputation was established quickly: as a gem to fly, or a fighter to be avoided, depending on whether one was an Allied or enemy pilot. In fact, it was more than a gem, for with its effective forward-firing synchronised machine gun, and the ability to remain manoeuvrable and responsive at a greater height than any contemporary fighter at the time of its introduction, it was also a killer. It was in great demand, and production totalled 1,770, the type being used also for home defence, many in this latter category with 100hp Gnome Monosoupape rotary engines, the resulting increase in rate of climb and overall performance making the Pup a most effective interceptor. In RNAS service the type played a significant pioneering role in the operation of aircraft from ships; one Pup flown by Sqn Cdr E H Dunning achieved the first landing on a ship under way at sea when he touched down on the deck of the aircraft carrier HMS *Furious* on August 2, 1917.

An attempt to capitalize on the superb flying qualities of the Pup was made in 1919 with development of the civil two-seat Dove, but its Le Rhône rotary engine was far from suitable for operation by a private pilot and this, more than any other factor, limited production to only 10 aircraft, most of them sold overseas.

Units Allocated

No. 1 Wing, RNAS, and Nos. 3, 4, 8, 9 and 12 (Naval) Squadrons (Western Front); Naval 'C' Squadron (Imbros); Seaplane Defence Flight (St Pol); RNAS coastal air stations at Dover, Great Yarmouth, Port Victoria and Walmer; RNAS training schools at Cranwell and Manston. Aircraft-carriers: *Argus*, *Campania*, *Furious* and *Manxman*. Warships with flying-off platforms: *Caledon*, *Cassandra*, *Cordelia*, *Dublin*, *Repulse* and *Yarmouth*.

TECHNICAL DATA - PUP

ENGINE: One 80hp le Rhône

WING SPAN: 26ft 6in

LENGTH: 19ft 3¾in

HEIGHT: 9ft 5in

WING AREA: 254 sq/ft

MAX SPEED: 111.5 mph at sea level

EMPTY WEIGHT: 787lb

LOADED WEIGHT: 1,225lb

CLIMB RATE: 16,100ft in 35min

SERVICE CEILING: 17,500ft

ENDURANCE: 3hrs

ARMAMENT: One forward-firing .303in Vickers machine-gun

Above: The world's first deck landing on an aircraft carrier was performed by Sqn Cdr E H Dunning on HMS *Furious* on August 2, 1917 in 'Ship' Pup N6452. Sadly, Dunning was killed on August 7 when the aircraft stalled on an overshoot and crashed into the sea.

Right: An excellent view of Sopwith 'Ship' Pup, N6454, being lifted through the forward hatch (aft of the forward flying-off deck) by a pair of 40ft-high wooden derricks during July 1917. The aircraft was one of three that were used during trials but, after delivery to the ship on July 11, the aircraft must have been damaged because, by July 21, the aircraft was 'deleted'.

Left: In 1919 Sopwith converted the last ten Pups on the production line into two-seat Doves for the civilian market. *Key Collection*

Below: The Pup was known officially as the Sopwith Scout and chronologically occupies a position between the 1½ Strutter and Triplane.

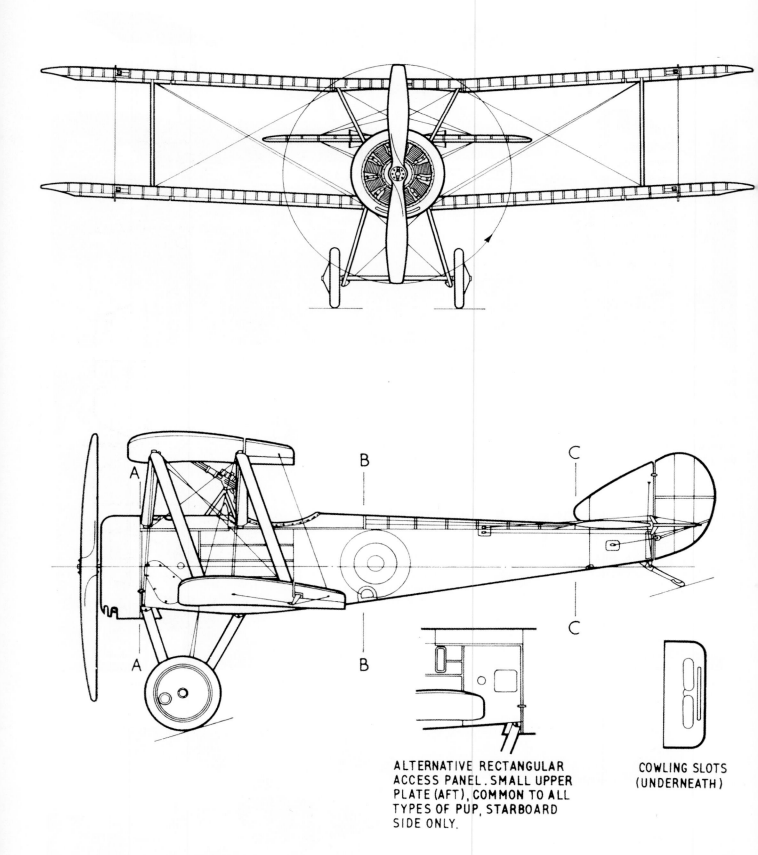

ALTERNATIVE RECTANGULAR
ACCESS PANEL. SMALL UPPER
PLATE (AFT), COMMON TO ALL
TYPES OF PUP, STARBOARD
SIDE ONLY.

COWLING SLOTS
(UNDERNEATH)

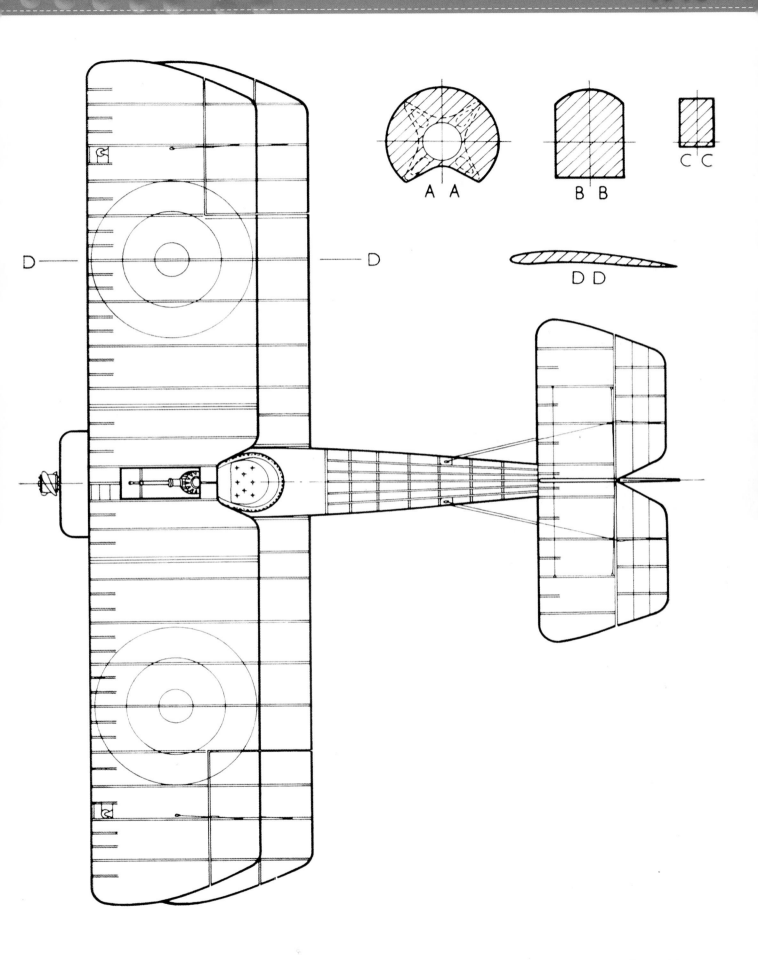

A A

B B

C C

D D

N5350 was the first machine of a batch of 40 aircraft ordered on July 23, 1916 under Contract CP.120945/16 and 87/A/1086, built by Clayton & Shuttleworth Ltd. After a brief period of service with the Design Flight at Eastchurch the Triplane joined 10 Naval Squadron, only to be lost off Boulogne, Northern France after the engine failed on April 23, 1917.

Complete ascendency with so few

» MAY 28, 1916
Maiden flight of prototype, N500

» DEC 1916
Triplane joins 1 Naval Air Squadron

» FEB 1917
8 Naval Air Squadron receives type

» JUN 27, 1917
Collishaw shoots down ace Allmenroder

» JUL 1917
Camel begins to replace Triplane

» OCT 19, 1917
Last Triplane, N5912 is delivered

The Sopwith Triplane was one of the great successes of the First World War. Its unusual configuration bestowed such qualities as a remarkable rate of roll and a fast climb, both invaluable in air combat. It was used only by the RNAS, and it gained complete ascendancy over the Western Front during the heavy aerial fighting of 1917.

In the Sopwith chronology the Triplane bridged the gap between the Pup and the Camel, and the first prototype (N500) performed Service trials with 'A' Fighting Squadron (Naval) at Furnes in June 1916. Production Triplanes entered service with No. 1 and 8 (Naval) Squadrons in February 1917 and with No. 10 (Naval) Squadron in May. Some remarkable engagements were fought by such redoubtable Triplane pilots as Sqn Cdr C D Booker, DSC, and Flt Sub Lt R A Little, of 'Naval Eight' and Flt Sub Lt Raymond Collishaw of 'Naval Ten'. The Triplanes of Collishaw's 'B' Flight (named *Black Death, Black Maria, Black Roger, Black Prince* and *Black Sheep*) became the terror of the enemy: between May and July 1917 they destroyed 87 German aircraft. Collishaw personally accounted for 16 in 27 days and shot down the German ace Karl Allmenröder on June 27.

The Triplane's career was glorious but brief. It remained in action for only seven months; in November 1917 the Camel had supplanted it in squadrons. Total deliveries to the RNAS amounted to around 140, including transfers from RFC contracts in exchange for naval Spads. Over 90 Triplanes were built by Sopwith to

meet original Admiralty contracts (N5420 to N5494 and N6290 to N6309); the rest came from subcontractors. The last Triplane (N5912), delivered on October 19, 1917, survives to the present day and is on display at the RAF Museum in London.

From February 1917 Triplanes had a smaller tailplane of 8ft span instead of the original Pup-type of 10ft span. This accompanied the change to a 130hp engine and improved diving characteristics.

Units Allocated
Nos. 1, 8, 9, 10 and 12 (Naval)Sqn on the Western Front. One aircraft (N5431) was used by 'E' Squadron of No. 2 Wing, RNAS, in Macedonia.

TECHNICAL DATA - TRIPLANE

ENGINE: One 130hp Clerget 9B	**MAX SPEED:** 117 mph at 5,000ft
WING SPAN: 26ft 6in	**CLIMB RATE:** 16,400ft in 26min 30sec
LENGTH: 18ft 10in	
HEIGHT: 10ft 6in	**SERVICE CEILING:** 20,500ft
WING AREA: 231 sq/ft	**ENDURANCE:** 2hrs 45min
EMPTY WEIGHT: 1,101lb	**ARMAMENT:** One .303in Vickers machine-gun
LOADED WEIGHT: 1,541lb	

The Sopwith Triplanes of 8 Naval Squadron pictured at Dunkirk sometime in 1917. Flt Cdr C H B Jenner-Parson's aircraft, N5468 *Angel* is pictured in the foreground. During its service with 8 Naval Squadron, the Triplane was credited with a single Albatros Scout and Aviatik kill; the latter was shared with two others.

Right: The capturing of an intact Sopwith Triplane was quite a prize for the Germans who immediately set about designing a triplane of their own. Every German aircraft manufacturer attempted to come up with an equivalent design and as a result at least 34 triplane prototypes were built including the Fokker V.4 which would lead to the Fokker Dr.I.

Below: N5364 was a Clayton & Shuttleworth-built machine which was delivered to 10 Naval Squadron on June 16, 1917. The Triplane was shot down by Ltn H Dilthey of Jasta 27 (then under the command of Lt Hermann Göring) on July 24, 1917. The pilot, Flt Sub-Lt T C May was killed when the aircraft's wings folded in a dive when it crashed south of Passchendaele.

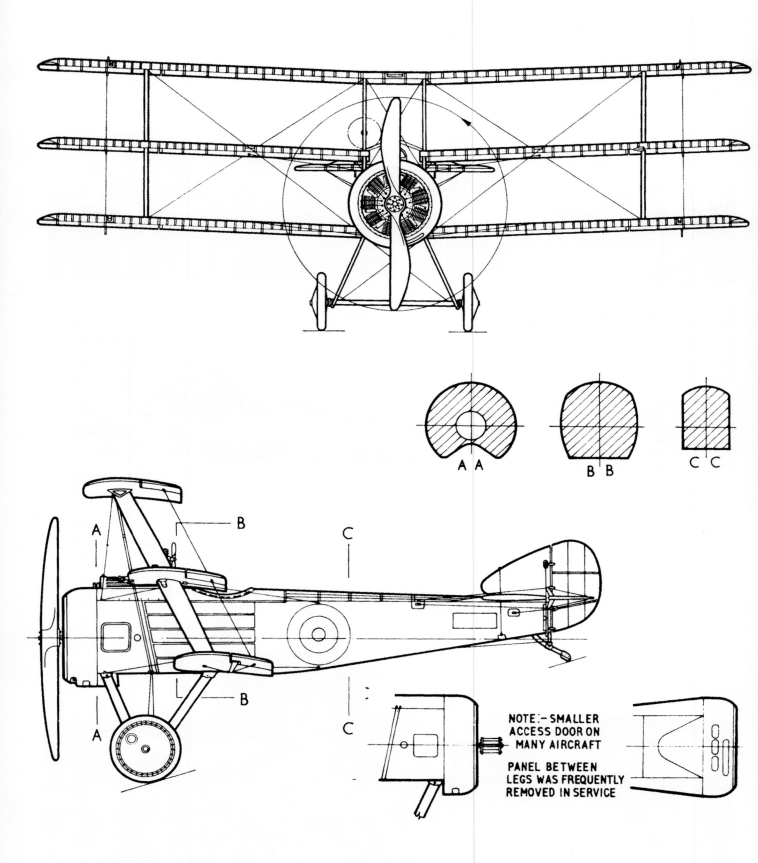

A A

B B

C C

A

B

C

B

A

A

C

C

NOTE:- SMALLER
ACCESS DOOR ON
MANY AIRCRAFT

PANEL BETWEEN
LEGS WAS FREQUENTLY
REMOVED IN SERVICE

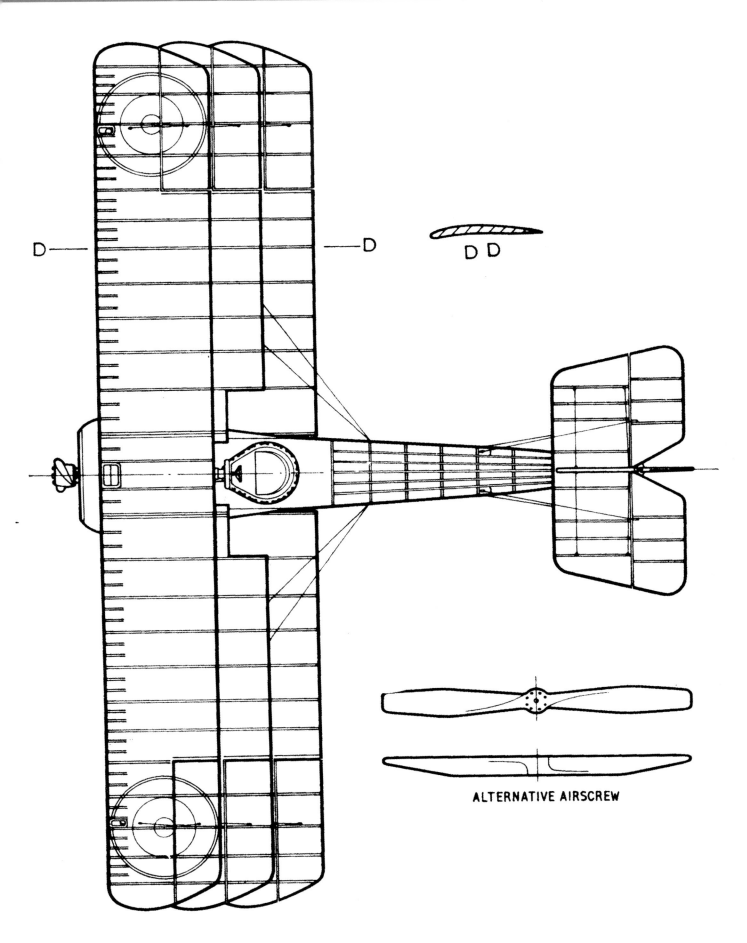

D — D

D D

ALTERNATIVE AIRSCREW

All the salient features of the LRT Tr, in the form in which it was completed, are shown in this view — notably, nacelle, wing and tail shape; landing gear; and mounting for Lewis gun behind rear cockpit.

>> **1916**
Maiden flight of the 'Egg-Box'

>> **1917**
Project abandoned

The Flying Eggbox

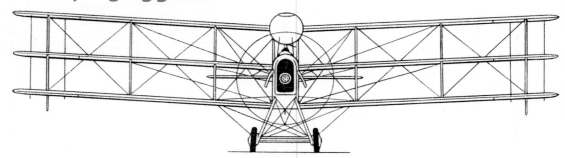

The LRT Tr., presumably signifying Long-Range Tractor Triplane, was designed to meet an RFC requirement for a combined escort fighter and airship interceptor. Other contenders were the Armstrong Whitworth F.K.6, also of triplane arrangement, and the Vickers FB.11, which was of more conventional biplane layout. Of bizarre appearance, the LRT Tr was a three-bay triplane with narrow-chord wings, all of which were fitted with ailerons. Power was provided by a 250hp Rolls-Royce

Eagle Mk I 12-cylinder water-cooled engine, and the crew comprised a pilot and two gunners. One gunner occupied the rear cockpit and the other a streamlined nacelle built around the upper wing centre section, both having a single 0.303in machine gun. By the time flight test commenced in 1916, it was appreciated that the concept of the LRT Tr had been rendered outdated by the advent of practical gun synchronisation equipment and the success against airships enjoyed by more conventional aircraft. This clumsy aeroplane, meanwhile assigned the epithet of 'Egg Box', was duly abandoned.

TECHNICAL DATA
L.R.T. TR.

ENGINE: One 250hp Rolls-Royce Eagle

WING SPAN: 52ft 9in

LENGTH: 35ft 3in

MAX SPEED: Approx. 107 mph

ARMAMENT: One .303in Lewis machine gun in upper nacelle and one .303in Lewis machine gun in rear cockpit

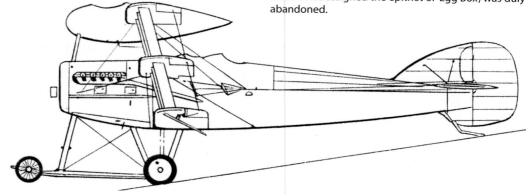

The Sopwith Bee was built in 1916 as a personal aircraft for Harry Hawker, Sopwith's chief test pilot. *Key Collection*

Harry Hawker's 'Tadpole'

Describing the Sopwith Bee is best left to a contemporary report, which amusingly details the machine as follows: 'The Bee was the smallest, and in some ways one of the most intriguing, of all the company's products. Woven round the little aeroplane by other old Sopwith hands were the usual stories of its having been 'chalked out on the shop floor by Harry Hawker to his own ideas'; though the contention that Hawker was indeed the moving spirit behind the design was so sustained, and so clearly plausible, as to admit but little doubt concerning his personal involvement.

'Meanwhile the airframe seems to merit more attention than is usually accorded it; that is, the mere notation that it embodied Pup components and that a curious feature of the tiny wings was that they were arranged to warp for lateral control instead of having ailerons.

'The feature, surely, that is even more striking is the form of centre section, which had a cut-out not only for the pilot's head, but another at the trailing edge. Thus it corresponded closely not only with the Dolphin (the tail - with its horn-balanced rudder - was likewise Dolphin-style), but with the Bulldog, Snail and Buffalo.

'Failing substantiation, this suggestion commands some further comment the 'fighter-style' opened-up centre section having already been accorded special notice. Now, how to reconcile this 'advanced' feature with such 'old-fashioned' ones as warping wings and a 50hp Gnome rotary?

'Aside from the ultra-short span and the wing-warping there was yet another feature of the Bee's wings that calls for remark, this being the narrowness of the gap - approximating to the chord of the wings themselves. Curious is the use of the term 'gap-chord' in the following - possibly corrupt - summary of an official report, issued very early in 1918: 'On the Effect of Cutting a Hole in the Top Plane of a Biplane. - Results of tests on the loss of lift of an R.A.F.6 biplane without fuselage, and with a gap-chord, due to the cutting of a hole in the top plane, the tests being carried out for analysis of incidence varying from 6° to plus 20°, and the results tabulated and plotted.'

'Though the seemingly well substantiated experimental fitment of a single Vickers gun would evidently have posed installation problems, the nature of the installation may have been unconventional - otherwise, indeed, the pilot's field of view might have been calamitously compromised. In any case, if synchronising gear of any kind were indeed fitted to the Gnome-powered Bee, some fairly extensive engine modifications would probably have been necessary.

'Speculative though much of the foregoing may be, the mere dimensions of the little aeroplane, are eloquent in themselves. Thus one muses finally on the name 'Tadpole' that was sometimes applied to this same machine.'

> **'THE FEATURE, SURELY, THAT IS EVEN MORE STRIKING IS THE FORM OF CENTRE SECTION, WHICH HAD A CUT-OUT NOT ONLY FOR THE PILOT'S HEAD, BUT ANOTHER AT THE TRAILING EDGE.'**

TECHNICAL DATA BEE

ENGINE: One Gnome Omega

WING SPAN: 16ft 3in

LENGTH: 14ft 3in

ARMAMENT: One Vickers .303in machine gun

One of many presentation Camels was D1922 which was 'Presented by Residents of Siam No.2' in early 1918. The aircraft joined 73 Squadron on May 23, 1918 and before its loss in September 1918, this Camel claimed three Fokker D.VIIIs, a single Fokker Dr.I and an unidentified two-seater, all in the hands of Lt R N Chandler.

The Finest British Fighter of the Great War

»» DEC 22, 1916
First flight by Harry Hawker at Brooklands

»» JUN 1917
Enters service with 4 Squadron

»» MAR 1918
First of seven HD squadrons equip with the Camel

»» APR 21, 1918
A Camel contributes to the demise of Manfred Von Richthofen

»» OCT 31, 1918
2,519 F.1 Camels are on RAF charge

»» JAN 1920
Withdrawn from the RAF

A replacement for the Sopwith Pup over the Western Front, the superb Camel was an outstanding fighter which is officially credited with shooting down 1,294 enemy aircraft and unofficially nearly 3,000.

A direct development of the Pup, the Camel was a heavier machine with a more powerful engine. The latter, along with the pilot, fuel and armament were concentrated into a very small area which gave the aircraft outstanding manoeuvrability, which when harnessed with experience was unrivalled by any opponent. Thanks to the right-hand torque of the engine, snap rolls to starboard could be performed in the blink of an eye. It was actually quicker to make a 90° turn to port by performing a three-quarter (270°) roll to starboard!

The Camel first entered service with 4 Squadron RNAS in June 1917 and in July also joined the RFC for the first time with 70 Squadron. Along with the SE.5a and the SPAD S.XIII the Camel helped to re-establish Allied air superiority until the middle of 1918. The type was also used as a Home Defence (HD) and night fighter and proved particularly effective against enemy Gothas from July 1917. The Camel was also usefully employed as a ground attack aircraft, dropping 25lb Cooper bombs and strafing enemy troops but would suffer a high number of losses in turn during these actions.

A total of 5,490 Camels were built and during its service the aircraft served with 50 RFC squadrons, eight RNAS squadrons, plus extensive service with the Australian Flying Corp, the Belgian Groupe de Chasses and four aero squadrons of the American Expeditionary Force.

Sopwith F.1 Camel C42 built by Nieuport & General Aircraft Co. Ltd of Cricklewood served with 226 Squadron where the name *The White Feather* was applied. The aircraft was later converted into a two-seater and saw service with the CFS at Upavon and the School of Aerial Fighting & Gunnery at Leuchars.

TECHNICAL DATA - F.1 CAMEL

ENGINE: One 130hp Clerget 9B

WING SPAN: 28ft

LENGTH: 18ft 9in

HEIGHT: 8ft 6in

WING AREA: 231 sq/ft

EMPTY WEIGHT: 930lb

LOADED WEIGHT: 1,455lb

MAX SPEED: 115 mph

CLIMB RATE: 1,085 ft/min

SERVICE CEILING: 21,000ft

ARMAMENT: Two forward-firing synchronised .303in Vickers machine-guns and up to four 25lb bombs carried externally

Evolved from the Pup, to which it bore a close family resemblance, the F.1 design - rapidly nicknamed Camel because of its hump-backed appearance, an epithet eventually to be recognised officially - was passed by the Sopwith experimental department on December 22, 1916.

The Camel first went into action with 70 Squadron in July 1917. By October 1918 Camels equipped a total of 32 RAF squadrons.

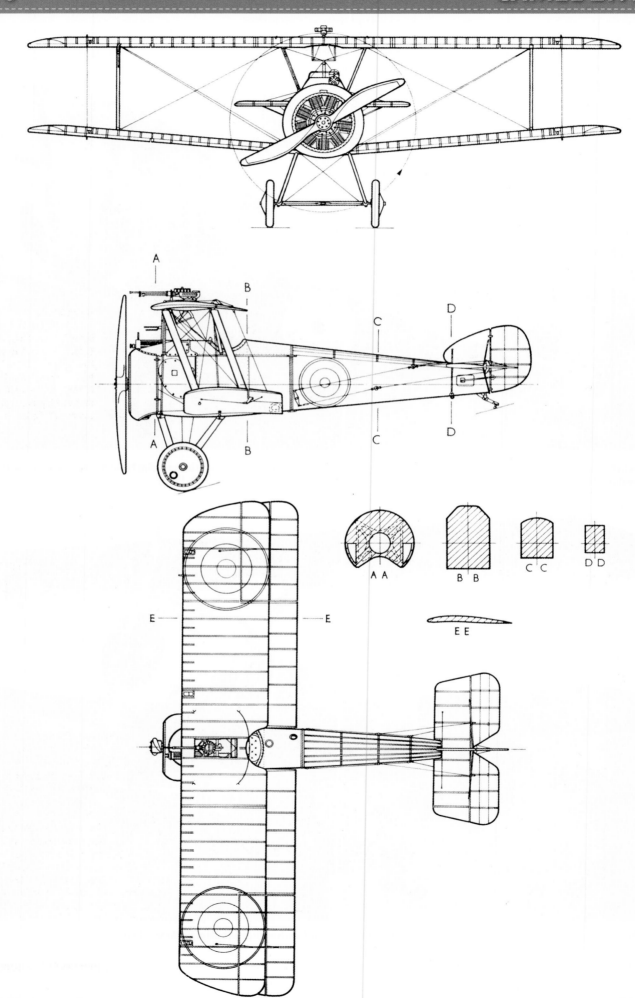

A A

B B

C C

D D

E E

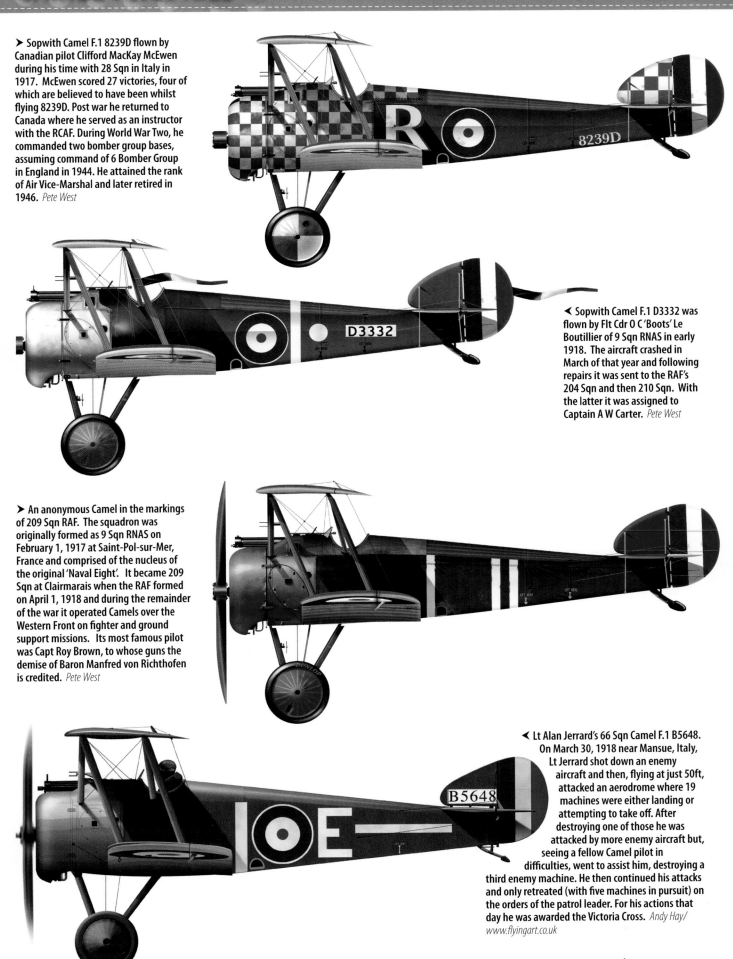

➤ Sopwith Camel F.1 8239D flown by Canadian pilot Clifford MacKay McEwen during his time with 28 Sqn in Italy in 1917. McEwen scored 27 victories, four of which are believed to have been whilst flying 8239D. Post war he returned to Canada where he served as an instructor with the RCAF. During World War Two, he commanded two bomber group bases, assuming command of 6 Bomber Group in England in 1944. He attained the rank of Air Vice-Marshal and later retired in 1946. *Pete West*

◄ Sopwith Camel F.1 D3332 was flown by Flt Cdr O C 'Boots' Le Boutillier of 9 Sqn RNAS in early 1918. The aircraft crashed in March of that year and following repairs it was sent to the RAF's 204 Sqn and then 210 Sqn. With the latter it was assigned to Captain A W Carter. *Pete West*

➤ An anonymous Camel in the markings of 209 Sqn RAF. The squadron was originally formed as 9 Sqn RNAS on February 1, 1917 at Saint-Pol-sur-Mer, France and comprised of the nucleus of the original 'Naval Eight'. It became 209 Sqn at Clairmarais when the RAF formed on April 1, 1918 and during the remainder of the war it operated Camels over the Western Front on fighter and ground support missions. Its most famous pilot was Capt Roy Brown, to whose guns the demise of Baron Manfred von Richthofen is credited. *Pete West*

◄ Lt Alan Jerrard's 66 Sqn Camel F.1 B5648. On March 30, 1918 near Mansue, Italy, Lt Jerrard shot down an enemy aircraft and then, flying at just 50ft, attacked an aerodrome where 19 machines were either landing or attempting to take off. After destroying one of those he was attacked by more enemy aircraft but, seeing a fellow Camel pilot in difficulties, went to assist him, destroying a third enemy machine. He then continued his attacks and only retreated (with five machines in pursuit) on the orders of the patrol leader. For his actions that day he was awarded the Victoria Cross. *Andy Hay/ www.flyingart.co.uk*

SHUTTLEWORTH'S INCREDIBLE CAMEL REPRODUCTION

Although a large number of replica Sopwith Camels have taken to the air over the last five decades, many of them bare only a passing resemblance to what is perhaps the most iconic of all Royal Flying Corps aircraft.

However, that all changed on May 18, 2017 when G-BZSC took to the skies over the world-famous Shuttleworth Collection in the hands of chief pilot 'Dodge' Bailey.

The successful maiden flight was the culmination of a 22-year-long project that was a collaboration between the Shuttleworth Trust and the Northern Aircraft Workshops (NAW) voluntary group, which until recently was based at Batley, West Yorkshire.

The first aircraft NAW produced for the Collection was a replica of a Clayton & Shuttleworth-built Sopwith Triplane. The aircraft was built to original 1916-era plans and fitted with an original 130hp Clerget rotary engine. It arrived at the Shuttleworth Collection's Old Warden airfield in June 1990 where it was assembled and painted to represent 'N6290'/*Dixie II* of 8 Naval Squadron. On seeing the quality and accuracy of the workmanship Sir Thomas Sopwith declared it to be a late production aircraft rather than a replica!

The team at NAW, which was founded by the late John Langham, then went on to complete a flyable Bristol M.1C replica for the Collection before it began work on the Camel F.1 in 1995.

The feasibility of the build came about when NAW co-coordinator Eric Barraclough, announced he had an almost complete set of Sopwith Camel drawings, which had been gifted to the society in the early 1970s along

The finished Camel sits proudly outside the Shuttleworth Collection hangars at Old Warden, Bedfordshire following an engine run in 2016. *All Darren Harbar*

with those for the Sopwith Triplane.

Their existence had mostly been forgotten about but combined with extensive research enabled the NAW team to begin constructing a highly accurate reproduction of the Camel.

The aircraft was built using traditional methods such as marking dye, scriber and file to commence making the many small metal fittings. Nearly all of the materials were sourced from the Shuttleworth Collection, including original wheels and fuel tanks.

The airframe itself is produced from high-grade spruce and birch ply, with the longerons and tailskid, made from airworthy grade ash. ➤

◄ Fitting the newly covered wings in the Shuttleworth engineering hangar.

▼ The Camel is equipped by a pair of replica .303in Vickers machines guns. On the original aircraft the guns were fitted with synchronising gear to enable them to fire through the propeller.

▲ The team at the Shuttleworth Collection keeps alive a host of skillsets that would otherwise be lost to the depths of history – not least the ability to cover aircraft in authentic fabric. Here, the Camel airframe gains its doped Irish Linen during 2014.

➤ This photograph of the Camel, taken as it underwent a trial assembly shortly after delivery from Yorkshire, shows the stunning workmanship employed by the volunteers at the Northern Aircraft Workshops.

The team at NAW had to build a fuselage jig before they could begin constructing the aircraft itself and once the fuselage sides were completed they were braced with piano wire as per the original Camel. A similar process followed with the four wings and centre section - all of which were assembled in jigs.

The entire build was overseen by the Light Aircraft Association and signed off by inspectors at every stage.

The project continued apace until 2013 when the group's lease on its premises at the former Yorkshire Motor Museum in Batley came to an end. That, combined with the average age of the volunteers, led NAW to disband at that point and the part-finished Camel was roaded to Old Warden on August 28 of that year for completion.

Once it was ensconced in Collection's workshops the Shuttleworth engineers continued the build and assembly, including splicing cables, installing the fuel and oil systems and covering the airframe in Irish Linen.

➤ Sitting in the Camel's cockpit is like a stepping into a time warp.

▲ The 140hp Clerget engine is run up to power during pre-flight testing.

➤ History is made as Dodge Bailey flies Camel G-BZSC/'D1851' for the first time on May 18, 2017.

An original 140hp Clerget rotary was also restored in Shuttleworth's engine workshop and finally the aircraft was painted to represent Camel 'D1851'. The original D1851 was built by Rushton Proctor and attached to 70 Sqn from 1918 and wore the inscription 'IKANOPIT' ("I can hop it").

After years of work at Old Warden the Camel – which, like the Triplane, is described as a late production version of the classic fighter – conducted its first engine runs on August 24, 2016. Finally, on May 18, 2017, the project reached a successful conclusion when 'Dodge' Bailey climbed away for a successful maiden flight.

Through the combined hard work of the NAW and Shuttleworth Collection has made it possible for airshow audiences to see a highly accurate rendition of a Camel performing in the skies of 2017 – exactly a century after the first examples entered service with the RFC.

Furthermore, the addition of the Camel to the Shuttleworth 'fleet' means it is the only place on the globe where visitors can see flyable examples of the Sopwith Pup, Triplane, Dove and now the Camel. ✧

SOPWITH B.1

This picture of the original B.1 gives the false impression that the upper-starboard aileron has a balancing surface.

» APR 1917
First of two prototypes flies from Brooklands

» APR/MAY 1918
Second prototype tested at Martlesham Heath

TECHNICAL DATA B.1

ENGINE: One 200hp Hispano-Suiza 8

WING SPAN: 38ft 6in

LENGTH: 27ft

HEIGHT: 9ft 6in

WING AREA: 460 sq/ft

EMPTY WEIGHT: 1,700lb

MAX TAKE-OFF WEIGHT: 3,055lb

MAX SPEED: 118.5 mph

CLIMB RATE: 10,000ft in 15min 30sec

ARMAMENT: One forward-firing .303in Lewis machine gun, up to 560lb in bombs which could include 20 x 28lb or 20 'French' 22lb bombs in the bomb bay

Experimental Bomber

In October 1916 Sopwith entered discussions with the Admiralty on the subject of two related proposals, one for a single-seat bomber and the other for a similar aircraft capable of carrying an 18in torpedo. The basis of the Sopwith proposals was the belief that both aircraft could be sufficiently small to avoid the necessity for folding wings. When, however, the Admiralty issued its formal requirement for a single-seat torpedo-bomber, the demand for sufficient fuel for four hours' flying at full throttle indicated the need for larger wings to provide more lift. The greater span thus demanded wing folding and, in order to avoid fouling the tail surfaces, a longer fuselage.

Admiralty interest in the smaller bomber project proved to be little more than academic and Sopwith decided to pursue it as a private venture, and managed to secure a licence to go ahead with a prototype basing the design on use of a 200hp Hispano-Suiza geared engine, in an installation similar to that being used in the second Sopwith Hispano Triplane fighter.

Thus the B.1 bomber design was in effect a scaled down version of the T.1 torpedo aircraft, but there the relationship ended. The longer fuselage of the bomber was dictated not by the span of the two-bay wings, but by the inclusion of a bomb bay located in the fuselage aft of the cockpit, capable of accommodating nine 50lb HE bombs, stowed vertically and suspended by their nose rings. However, further discussions with the Admiralty elicited the information that the RNAS in France was interesting in using the French 10kg 'liquid-anilite' bomb and after release from the aircraft, a small wind-driven vane ruptured the separating diaphragm, allowing the elements to mix and thus 'arming' the highly sensitive explosive compound. No impact detonator was therefore required as an alternative to the British bomb. In order to cater for 20

of these weapons the bomb suspension beams in the Sopwith were moved further apart by about two inches.

The B.1 prototype, believed to have been numbered X.6, was first flown at Brooklands early in April 1917 and underwent brief assessment at the Isle of Grain soon after. During these trials the aircraft was loaded with twenty 10kg anilite bombs and, at an all-up weight of 2,945lb, returned a maximum speed of 118.5 mph at 10,000ft.

Although this was regarded as exceptionally good performance, the B.1 was criticised for its lack of longitudinal control, being found to be tail heavy while carrying the full bomb load, and nose heavy when flying light, a lack of trim that could not be fully countered, even with the adjustable tailplane at its limits of travel. The ailerons were also criticised, though probably owing to undue friction in the control circuits.

Nevertheless the Admiralty stepped in and purchased this aircraft and it was delivered to the RNAS 5 Wing at Dunkerque for Service trials, participating in raids by the naval squadrons flying from Petite Synthe and Coudekerque alongside their DH.4s. During these operations the B.1 was armed with a single synchronised Lewis gun mounted above the engine.

On return to Britain, the engine was removed and returned to Kingston, while the airframe was delivered to the Admiralty's Experimental Construction Depot at Port Victoria. Here it was rebuilt as a two-seat naval reconnaissance aircraft; as such it became the prototype of the Grain Griffin and given the experimental naval serial number N50.

This second aeroplane was also purchased by the Admiralty as B1496 and underwent further trials by Service pilots. However, no further interest appears to have been expressed in the project and the ultimate fate of this aircraft is not known.

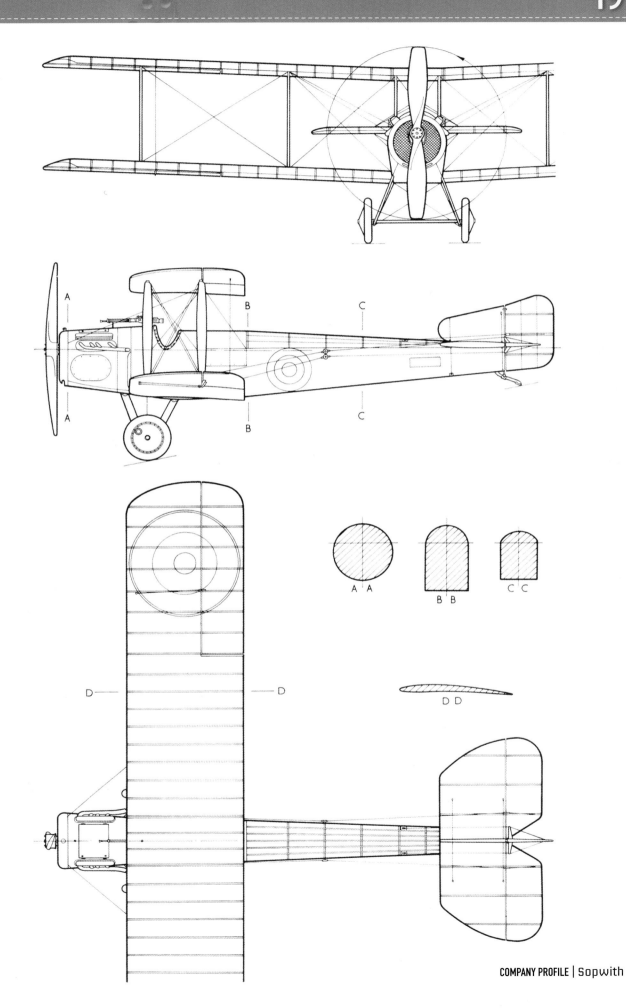

The Hippo two-seat fighter was a counterpart of the Salamander and a contemporary of the Rhino. The first machine was fitted with a pair of rocking-pillar mountings for two Lewis guns and the second had a Scarff ring-mounting for a single Lewis gun.

Providing the Best View for Pilot and Gunner

» **APR 30, 1917**
Company drawings are approved

» **SEP 13, 1917**
Prototype maiden flight

» **FEB 1918**
Military interest in Hippo ends

Built as a private venture, the Hippo two-seat fighter featured negative wing stagger, the gap between the wings being completely filled by the deep fuselage, and the first of two prototypes was flown on September 13, 1917. A two-bay biplane powered by a 200hp Clerget 11Eb 11-cylinder rotary, the Hippo had an armament of two fixed synchronised 0.303in and (initially) two free-mounted guns of similar calibre, or (later) one 0.303in gun on a Scarff mount in the rear cockpit. Official trials were performed at Martlesham Heath in January 1918, these having been delayed by engine problems. The performance of the Hippo was considered inferior to that of the Bristol F.2B and lateral control was criticised, and, on February 2, 1918, the aircraft was returned to Sopwith. Despite official rejection, the manufacturer fitted new wings, plain ailerons and an enlarged fin. Wing dihedral was increased and stagger was reduced, and with these modifications the Hippo re-emerged in April 1918, with a second prototype following in June. By that time, the

F.2B was giving satisfaction in service and it became apparent to Sopwith that the Hippo was too late, further development being discontinued. The following data relate to the Hippo in its original form.

TECHNICAL DATA - HIPPO

ENGINE: One 200hp Clerget 11Eb

WING SPAN: 38ft 9in

LENGTH: 24ft 6in

HEIGHT: 9ft 4in

WING AREA: 340 sq/ft

EMPTY WEIGHT: 1,481lb

LOADED WEIGHT: 2,590lb

MAX SPEED: 115 mph at 10,000ft

CLIMB RATE: 1,000 ft/min

ARMAMENT: Two forward-firing .303in Vickers machine guns and one Lewis on a Scarff ring in the rear cockpit

The chronic troubles that beset the the Cobham's A.B.C. Dragonfly engine caused the first machine, H671, to be fitted with high-compression Siddeley Pumas, and thus to be designated Cobham Mk II.

Sopwith's Only Twin-Engined Bomber

Notable as being the only twin-engine Sopwith aeroplane ever built, the triplane Cobham's career was also bedevilled by its association with the ABC Dragonfly engines. Designed during the summer of 1918 to the Air Ministry Specification IV, as qualified in Specifications VI and VIII by virtue of variations in range and bomb load (all three of which were amalgamated in the Department of Research Type 3 Specification) - the Cobham began building in September that year.

Although the aircraft was designed as a three-seat medium bomber, capable of carrying three 250lb bombs (stowed internally and suspended vertically), the greater part of the Cobham's life was preoccupied with attempts to come to terms with the thoroughly unreliable Dragonfly. The first of three prototypes ordered, H671, was completed at Brooklands in about December 1918 but, owing to delays in the delivery of the 320hp Dragonfly I engines, Herbert Smith (whose design the Cobham was) was instructed to make provision to install a pair of standard 240hp Siddeley Puma engines, so as to begin flight trials as quickly as possible. H671 was therefore termed the Cobham Mark II, and was flown in about April 1919. It was, however, never destined to receive Dragonfly engines as, sometime in 1919, it suffered an accident and was undergoing repair at about the time that the first modified Dragonfly IA engines were starting delivery. It was therefore fitted with high-compression Pumas and underwent performance trials with these at Martlesham Heath in March 1920, and in November that year was delivered to the RAE, Farnborough, where it was last flown on January 27, 1921.

Neither of the other two Cobhams was flown during 1919; these, termed Mark Is, were both powered by 360hp Dragonfly IAs with redesigned cylinders and pistons. H672 and H673 were first flown in January and February 1920 respectively but, with the Sopwith company beginning to suffer serious financial difficulty, they were taken on Air Ministry charge and delivered to Martlesham Heath in February. Recurring engine failures caused them to be forwarded on to Farnborough to await a decision on the future of the Dragonfly and, when its development was abandoned in September, the Cobham Is were struck off Air Ministry charge.

The Cobham's airframe design underwent fairly extensive change when it was discovered that the Dragonfly was substantially over the weight originally notified to Sopwith; compared with the original works drawings of the aircraft, the Mark I prototypes had their engines set some fifteen inches further aft, with the plane of the cylinder centreline in line with the centre wing's leading edge. Moreover, the Mark Is featured changes in wing stagger, the top wings being rigged with positive stagger, and no stagger on the bottom wings; the Puma-powered Mark II featured slight sweepback and back stagger on the top wing. The Mark I was also found to require increased rudder area, this being extended below the fuselage sternpost, with horn balances at each end. This modification was said to have been demanded by Harry Hawker who, having had to land a Cobham with one dead engine, found the aircraft almost unmanageable and entirely devoid of rudder control.

TECHNICAL DATA
COBHAM MK I & MK II

ENGINE: (I) Two 360hp A.B.C. Dragonfly IA; (II) Two 290hp Siddeley Puma

WING SPAN: 54ft

LENGTH: 38ft

HEIGHT: 13ft

WING AREA: 271 sq/ft

GROSS WEIGHT: 6,300lb

ARMAMENT: Two .303in Vickers machine guns on a Scarff ring in the nose and dorsal position and up to 750lb in bombs

>> **APR 1919**
Dragonfly-powered prototype flies

>> **JAN/FEB 1920**
Maiden flights of H672 & H673

>> **JAN 27, 1921**
Mk II final flight

SOPWITH SNIPE

A 43 Squadron Snipe with an under-fuselage bomb carrier. *Aeroplane*

>> **OCT 1917**
Maiden flight of first prototype

>> **SEP 1918**
Snipe in action on the Western Front

>> **OCT 27, 1918**
Barker wins the Victoria Cross

>> **1923**
Canadian Air Force retires Snipe

>> **MAY 1926**
43 Sqn retires Snipe

>> **1928**
Snipe obsolete in RAF service

Helping to Carry the RAF into Peace

Introduced as a successor to the famous Sopwith Camel, the Sopwith Snipe first reached the RAF on the Western Front in September 1918. In the three months before the war's end it proved itself to be the best of the Allied fighters, though less than a hundred made it into action. It was whilst flying a Snipe that Maj W G Barker DSO and bar, MC and 2 bars, fought his celebrated single-handed engagement with fifteen Fokker D.VIIIs on October 27, 1918, for which he was awarded the Victoria Cross.

Owing to the financial limitations forced on the RAF in the early post-war years, the Snipe remained with RAF fighter squadrons until as late as 1926. By then, as a typical rotary-engine scout of the First World War period, it was an undoubted anachronism among the Siskins, Woodcocks and Grebes which had begun to replace it from 1924. From April 1920 to November 1922, the Snipes of 25 Squadron, stationed at Hawkinge, Kent, represented the sole fighter defence of the United Kingdom. The last Snipes on Home Defence duties were those of 43 Squadron at Henlow, replaced by Gamecocks in May 1926.

Overseas, Snipes remained in Iraq until 1 Squadron disbanded in November 1926. At Flying Training Schools Snipes remained in service after this date, and about forty were used as two-seat dual-control trainers.

Snipes were regular performers at the RAF Display at Hendon from its inception in 1920, and they made their last appearance with 17 Squadron in 1926. One of the highlights of the 1921 show was a polished demonstration of formation aerobatics by Snipes of the Central Flying School led by Sqn Ldr C Draper, DSC.

Wartime production orders for 4,500 Snipes suffered heavy cancellations (or were changed to Dragon and Nighthawk orders) with the end of hostilities, by which time only 288 Snipes had left the factories. However, production continued into 1919, ending by September when over 2,000 had been completed, many to go into storage and never to enter service.

Snipes which gave wartime service were predominantly from the original Sopwith-built batch, E7987-E8266. Those completed post-war (many by the wide range of sub-contractors used) were in the ranges E6137-E6656, E6787-E6921, E6937-E7036, E7337-E7836, E7987-E8286, E8307-E8406, F2333-F2532, H351-H650, H4865-H4916, H8663-H8707, J451-J475 and J6493-J6522. In 1921, the RAF had 532 Snipes on strength, including nearly 400 in storage. Over the period 1919 to 1926, the Snipe served on twenty RAF squadrons and was not finally declared obsolete until 1928.

Unit Allocations

Home: Nos 3 (Manston and Upavon), 17 and 25 (Hawkinge), 19, 29 and 111 (Duxford), 23 (Henlow), 32 (Kenley), 37 (Biggin Hill), 41 (Northolt), 43 (Spittlegate and Henlow), 56 (Hawkinge and Biggin Hill), 70 (Spittlegate), 78 (Sutton's Farm), 112 (Throwley), 143 (Detling), 201 (Lake Down), and 208 (Netheravon). Overseas: Nos 1 (India and Iraq), 3 (India), 25 (Constantinople), 56 and 80 (Egypt). France (1918-19): Nos 43, 80, 201 and 208. Germany (1918-19): Nos 70 and 208.

Although outdated by that time, the Snipe remained in RAF service until 1926.

TECHNICAL DATA - SNIPE

ENGINE: One 200hp Bentley BR.2

WING SPAN: 31ft 1in

LENGTH: 19ft 10in

HEIGHT: 9ft 6in

WING AREA: 271 sq/ft

EMPTY WEIGHT: 1,312lb

LOADED WEIGHT: 2,020lb

MAX SPEED: 121 mph at 10,000ft

SERVICE CEILING: 19,500ft

ENDURANCE: 3hrs

RATE OF CLIMB: 15,000ft in 18min 50sec

ARMAMENT: Two .303in Vickers machine guns and up to four 25lb bombs

Above: One of the most famous incidents in which the Snipe was involved, occurred on October 27, 1918 when 201 Sqn pilot Maj William G Barker engaged the enemy in Snipe E8102. Barker attacked a two-seater German aircraft and swiftly shot it down but was soon attacked by a formation of at least 15 Fokker D.VIIs. He was wounded three times, twice losing consciousness momentarily, but managed to shoot down at least three D.VIIs before making a forced landing on the Allied lines. Barker was awarded the Victoria Cross for this actions and the fuselage of his Snipe is preserved in his native Canada. *Andy Hay/www.flyingart.co.uk*

A variety of late First World War and post-war types on parade at RAF Halton on June 3, 1923 including Snipes, E7716 and E7545.

SOPWITH SNIPE

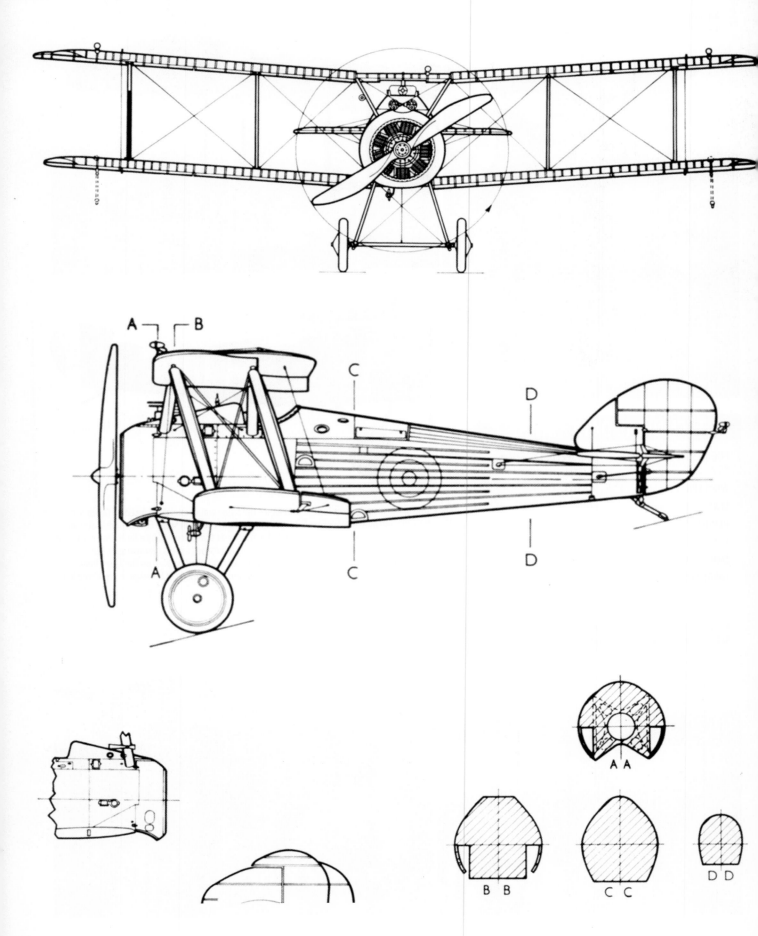

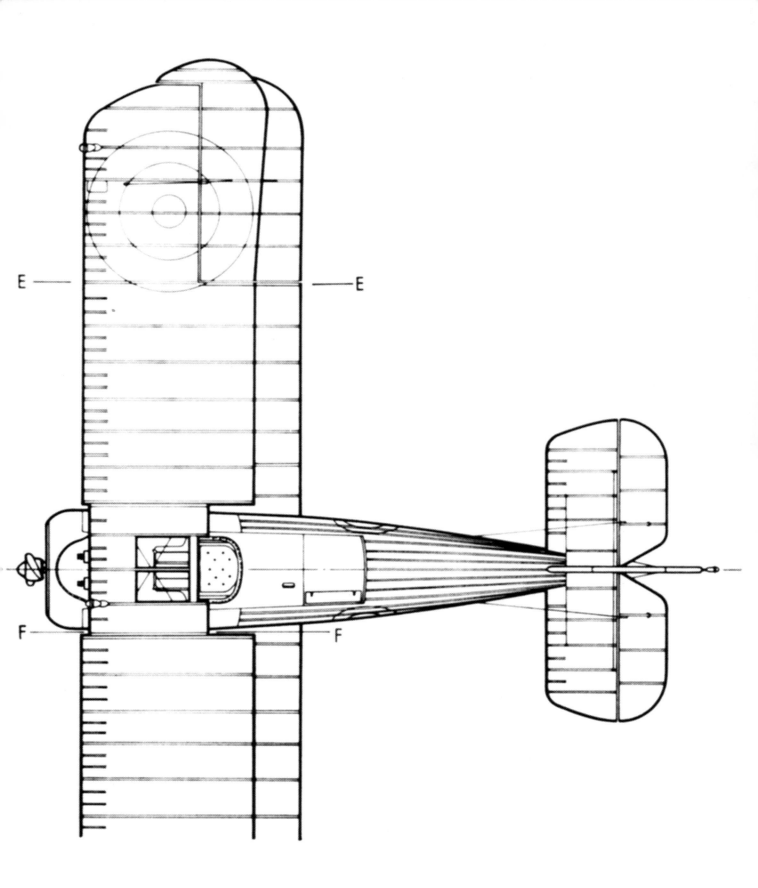

E — — — E

F — — F

The Dragon was a development of the Snipe fitted with the 360hp ABC Dragonfly IA radial engine in place of the BR.2 rotary. The prototype (E7990) was a converted Snipe and was followed by a batch of production aircraft during 1919, but the type never entered squadron service with the RAF.

» APR 1918
Maiden flight of first prototype

» OCT 16, 1918
Snipe contract switched to Dragon

» JUN 7, 1919
Dragons begin to go into long-term storage

» APR 1923
Dragon declared obsolete

Troubled Snipe development

The sixth and last prototype of the Snipe was fitted with the 320hp ABC Dragonfly nine-cylinder radial engine as the Snipe Mk II. Despite the shortcomings of this engine, it endowed the Snipe with an outstanding performance when it could be persuaded to function efficiently and, with the Dragonfly's faults still to be recognised as incurable, 30 Snipe Mk IIs were ordered with the ABC engine on May 3, 1918. Assigned the name Dragon, these were delivered in June and July 1919, the production prototype having appeared in the previous January. The Dragonfly-engined Snipes were produced in parallel with aircraft built from the ground up as Dragons, these having horn-balanced upper ailerons and the 360hp Dragonfly Ia engine, armament comprising the standard pair of synchronised 0.303in machine guns.

In the United Kingdom, development work on the Dragonfly engine (and production likewise) continued after the Armistice; and though the Sopwith Dragon was certainly deemed to be a standard RAF fighter in 1921 it never equipped a squadron before being declared obsolete in April 1923. Nor does the intended unarmed two-seater version, which Sopwith had designed by April 1920, seem to have materialised. The absence of armament on a modified production-type Dragon at the Royal Aircraft Establishment - the aircraft being fitted with heater-muffs on the carburettor air-intakes jointly with drooping exhaust tail-pipes which collected from the lower group of cylinders - having no apparent connection with this variant.

Though a number of Nieuport Nighthawks (originally designed for the Dragonfly engine) were later re-engined with either the nine-cylinder Bristol Jupiter or the fourteen-cylinder Armstrong Siddeley Jaguar radial, Sopwith Dragons were not so converted. Even so, it is worth noting that the original two-bay form of the Hawker Woodcock (circa 1923) was fitted with an engine of each type, and that in tail design, as well as in other respects, bore a resemblance to Sopwith's decidedly reluctant Dragon.

The number of Dragons completed is not known, but all were Sopwith-built, the orders placed with the company being: F7001-F7030 and J3617-J3916. Some airframe parts may have been used for Snipes or Salamanders, and orders for many Dragons from other companies were cancelled.

TECHNICAL DATA - DRAGON

ENGINE: One 360hp ABC IA	**GROSS WEIGHT:** 2,132lb
WING SPAN: 31ft 1in	**MAX SPEED:** 150 mph
LENGTH: 21ft 9in	**SERVICE CEILING:** 25,000ft
HEIGHT: 9ft 6in	**ARMAMENT:** Two .303in
WING AREA: 271 sq/ft	Vickers machine guns

About 200 of a 300-aircraft contract were completed and efforts to cure the engine's troubles continued until the autumn of 1921. The Dragon, although officially adopted at that time as a standard RAF single-seat fighter, was never issued to a squadron and the type was officially declared obsolete in April 1923.

Left: The Dragonfly-engined Snipes were produced in parallel with aircraft built from the ground up as Dragons.

Originally 300 7F.1 Snipes were ordered under Contract No.35a/3480/C4083 on October 16, 1918 but this order was changed to the Dragon on November 21, 1918. J3704 was one of 100 aircraft placed in long-term storage from June 7, 1919.

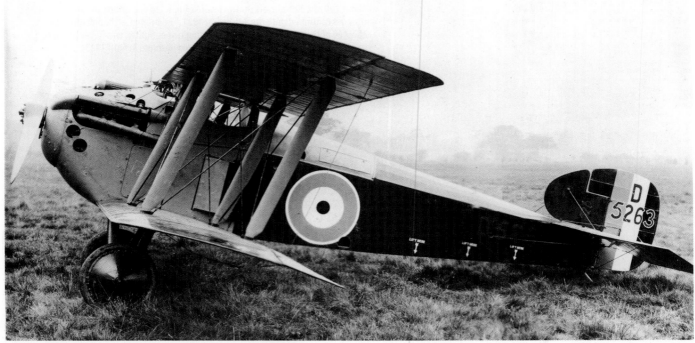

Designed to provide the pilot with the best possible view in tactically important directions, the 5F.1 Dolphin was unusual in being a two-bay equi-span biplane with negative stagger.

MAY 23, 1917
Maiden flight of the Dolphin

JUN 28, 1917
Order placed for 200 Dolphins

OCT 1917
Series production commences

FEB 1918
Enters service with 19 & 79 Squadrons

MAR 1919
23 Squadron retires type

1923
Dolphin retires from Second Polish Republic Air Force

The World's First Multi-Gun Single-Seat Fighter

The Sopwith 5F.1 Dolphin was an unusual single-seat fighter biplane built around a deep-section fuselage with the upper wing mounted close to it. Designed to give its pilot the best possible field of view, the pilot's head projected through a gap in the centre-section - thus allowing a superb upward and all-round view, although at a cost of some restriction in the view below. Armament consisted of two fixed synchronised 0.303in guns and either one or two guns of similar calibre mounted over the wing centre section and movable, but usually firing forwards and upwards. Powered by a 200hp Hispano-Suiza geared eight-cylinder water-cooled engine, the prototype was flown for the first time in May 1917 and, following satisfactory tests, began to enter service as the Dolphin Mk I towards the end of the year. The first Dolphin squadron was deployed to France in February 1918, and the decision was taken to licence-build a version for the US Air Service in France.

Two versions with alternative engines were numbered among the 1,532 Dolphins produced, only 621 of this total entering service before the war ended, the remainder placed in storage. They comprised Dolphin Mk Is with the same geared engine as the prototype, but failure of the drive gears led to introduction of the Dolphin Mk III with a similarly-powered direct-drive version of the Hispano-Suiza engine. The designation Dolphin Mk II was allocated to a version with a 300hp Hispano-Suiza direct-drive engine which was to be manufactured by the SACA (Société Anonyme des Constructions Aéronautiques) and the Air Service anticipated taking delivery of 2,194 by mid-1919. In the event, only a few Dolphin Mk IIs were completed before the Armistice prompted cancellation of all remaining contracts. Difficulties with the reduction

gear of the original 200hp engine led to the conversion of many to direct drive, aircraft fitted with the modified power plant being designated Dolphin Mk III with some having their engine's compression ratio raised to boost output to some 220hp.

The Dolphin was not particularly popular with pilots, for its back-staggered wing induced unusual stall characteristics, and the pilot's exposed position could prove fatal in a nose-over following a bad landing. In consequence some aircraft used by training units were given 'crash pylons' above the centre-section, and Dolphins adopted for a night-flying role had similar pylons above the wing. In addition to their use by the RFC and RAF, No.1 Squadron of the Canadian Air Force trained with the type but the war ended before they became operational, and five were acquired by the American Expeditionary Force for evaluation.

Production of the Dolphin totalled 1,532 aircraft, of which all but 121 were built during 1918. Both Dolphin Mks I and III were finally withdrawn from RAF service by mid-1919.

TECHNICAL DATA - DOLPHIN MK I

ENGINE: One 200hp Hispano-Suiza 8B

WING SPAN: 32ft 6in

LENGTH: 22ft 3in

HEIGHT: 8ft 6in

WING AREA: 263 sq/ft

EMPTY WEIGHT: 1,410lb

MAX TAKE-OFF WEIGHT: 1,959lb

MAX SPEED: 131 mph at sea level

SERVICE CEILING: 20,000ft

RANGE: 195 miles

RATE OF CLIMB: 10,000ft in 12min 5sec

ARMAMENT: Two .303in Vickers machine guns and up to two .303in Lewis machine guns and up to four 25lb bombs

S. 189.   SOPWITH DOLPHIN NIGHT FLYER — TYPE E.E.1.   FEB. 19/18.

Above: Primarily of fabric-covered wire-braced wooden construction with an upper centre section of steel tube, the Dolphin was powered by a 200hp Hispano-Suiza geared eight-cylinder water-cooled engine in its initial production form.

Right: The prototype was flown in late May 1917, the first production contract was placed the following month, on June 29, and deliveries to the RFC began late in the year.

Below: Armament consisted of two fixed and synchronised 0.303in guns and either one or two guns of similar calibre mounted over the wing centre section.

SOPWITH DOLPHIN

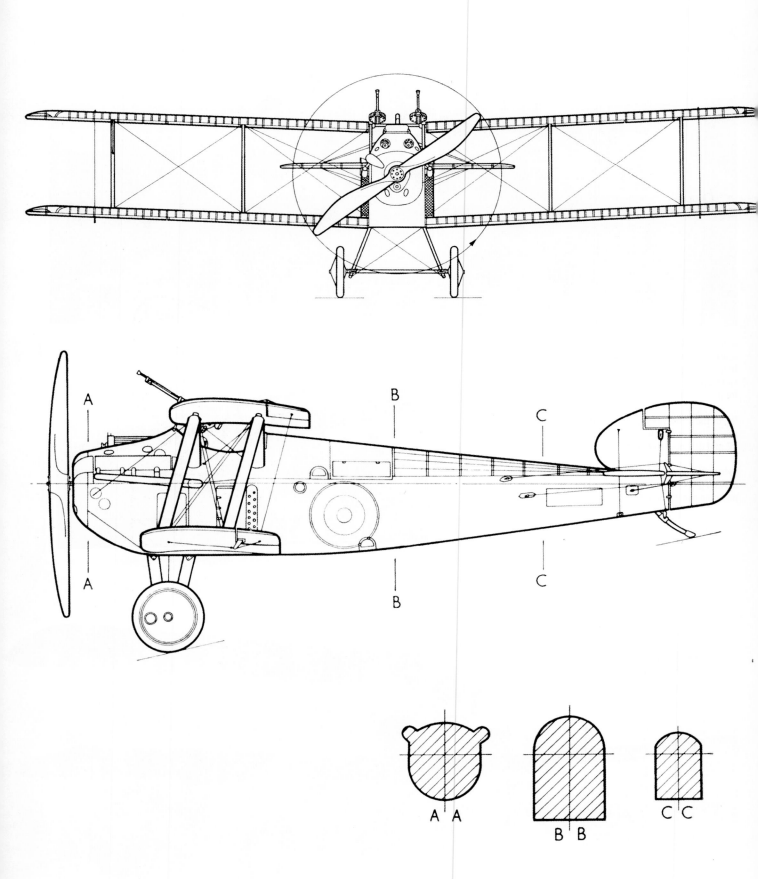

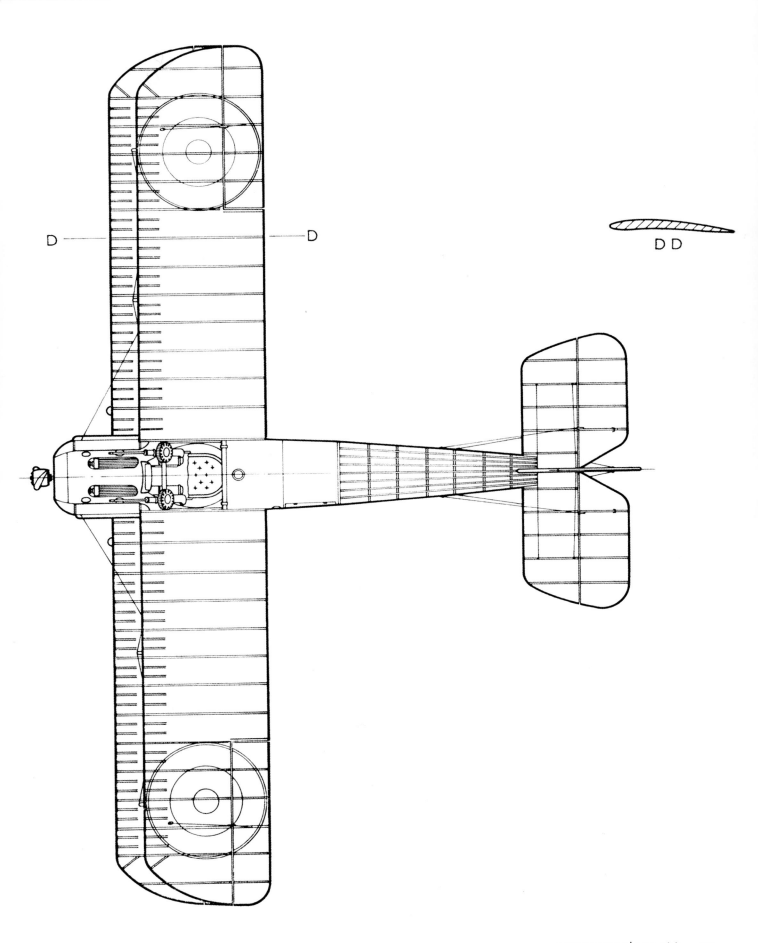

D ——————————— D

D D

SOPWITH TF.2 SALAMANDER

A derivative of the Snipe, the Salamander was intended for ground-attack duties, and for this purpose carried 650lb of armour plate for the protection of the pilot and petrol tanks. This example, F6533, is pictured at McCook Field in the USA.

<< **APR 27, 1918**
Maiden flight of TF.2 from Brooklands

<< **MAY 19, 1918**
Prototype TF.2 wrecked

<< **JUN 18, 1918**
Initial production order placed

<< **NOV, 1918**
Salamander enters RAF service

<< **1919**
Camouflage trials

<< **1922**
Last examples in Egypt

Armoured Ground-Attack

A requirement for an armoured single-seat ground-attack fighter was issued to the Sopwith Company in January 1918, a standard F.1 Camel being rapidly fitted with armour protection and triple-gun armament, and flying as the TF.1 in the following month (T.F. indicating Trench Fighter). For use in a ground-attack role against enemy trenches, the Salamander TF.2 was developed from the Snipe, but had some 650lb of armour plate beneath the forward fuselage to protect the pilot and fuel tanks from ground fire.

The TF.1 was a stop-gap type that could be made available rapidly by modifying existing aircraft, but the requirement had specified the use of a 230hp Bentley BR.2 nine-cylinder rotary engine and Sopwith discarded the TF.1 in favour of a modified Snipe design as the TF.2 Salamander. Despite many similarities to the Snipe, the Salamander differed extensively and there was little or no interchangeability between the two. The forward portion of the fuselage was a simple armoured box, the bottom being 11mm plate, the sides 6-mm plate, the front - the engine backplate - 8mm plate and the rear 10mm plate with a second 6mm plate separated by 3.75in. Armament comprised two synchronised 0.303in guns with provision for four 25lb bombs. The first of three prototypes was flown on April 27, 1918,

and the Salamander was ordered in large numbers (contracts were placed with the parent company, Air Navigation Co, Glendower Aircraft, National Aircraft, Palladium Autocars and Wolseley Motors), 37 being on RAF charge by October 31. When hostilities ceased, production of the Salamander continued with a view to its use by the post-war RAF, and by mid-1919, when manufacture eventually terminated, Sopwith had delivered 334 and other contractors had contributed a further 85.

The Salamander only briefly served with two operational RAF squadrons, namely 96 Squadron from November to December 9, 1918 and 157 Squadron, from November 1918 to February 1, 1919.

TECHNICAL DATA - SALAMANDER

ENGINE: One 230hp Bentley BR.2	**MAX SPEED:** 125 mph at 500ft
WING SPAN: 31ft 2 5/8in	**SERVICE CEILING:** 13,000ft
LENGTH: 19ft 6in	
HEIGHT: 9ft 4in	**ENDURANCE:** 1hr 20mins
WING AREA: 272 sq/ft	**ARMAMENT:** Two .303in Vickers
EMPTY WEIGHT: 1,844lb	machine guns and four 25lb
LOADED WEIGHT: 2,512lb	bombs

Above: F6602, with strut-braced tailplane and horn-balanced top ailerons, was photographed on January 25, 1919.

Right: Production orders for the Salamander were: Sopwith E5429-E5431; F6501-F7000. A few in the range J5892-J5991 were completed by Glendower Aircraft Co Ltd, but large Salamander orders placed with the Air Navigation Co Ltd, National Aircraft Factory No.1, Palladium Autocars Ltd and Wolseley Motors Ltd were cancelled or curtailed by reason of the Armistice.

Below: The first prototype (E5429) pictured on May 1, 1918, flew service trials on the Western Front. About forty had been delivered to the RAF by the Armistice.

TF.2 SALAMANDER

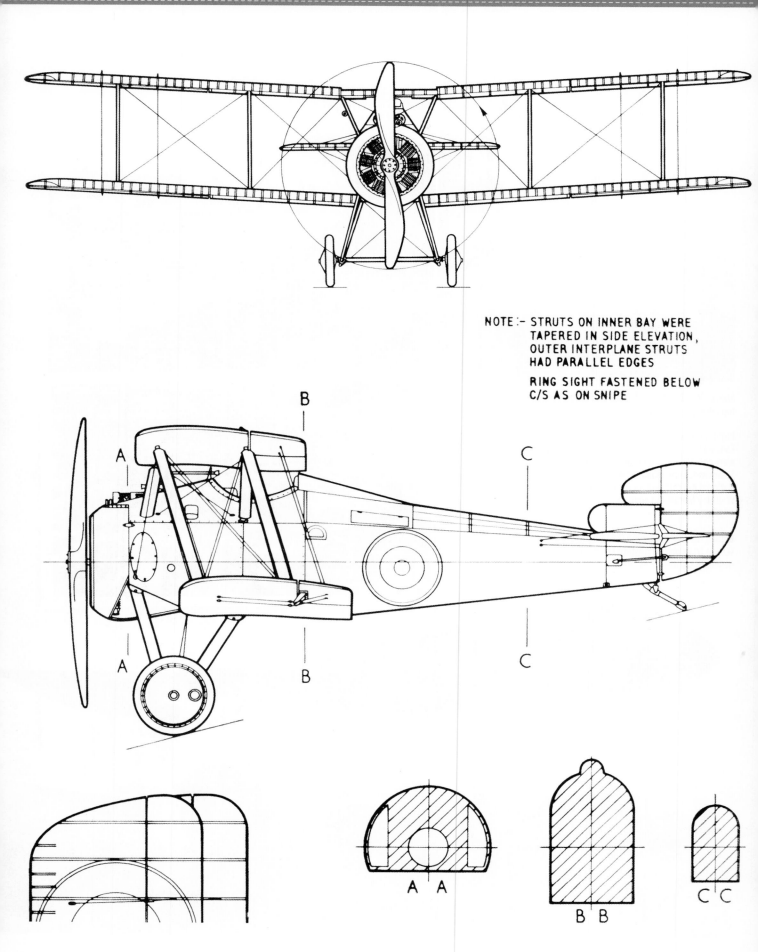

NOTE :– STRUTS ON INNER BAY WERE
TAPERED IN SIDE ELEVATION,
OUTER INTERPLANE STRUTS
HAD PARALLEL EDGES

RING SIGHT FASTENED BELOW
C/S AS ON SNIPE

A

B

C

A A

B B

C C

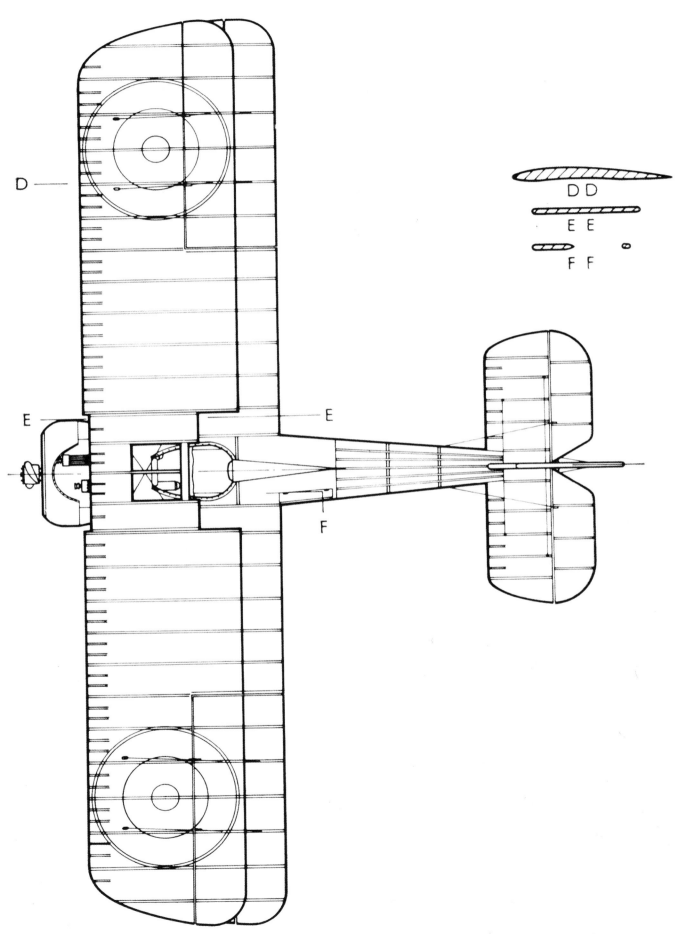

D

E

E

F

D D

E E

F F

The Cuckoo was something of a landmark in British naval aircraft design; it was the first landplane torpedo-carrier capable of operation from a flying-off deck.

TECHNICAL DATA
CUCKOO

ENGINE: One 200hp Sunbeam Arab V8

WING SPAN: 46ft 9in

LENGTH: 28ft 6in

HEIGHT: 10ft 8in

WING AREA: 566 sq/ft

EMPTY WEIGHT: 2,199lb

LOADED WEIGHT: 3,883lb

MAX SPEED: 105.5 mph

SERVICE CEILING: 12,100ft

RANGE: 291 miles

ARMAMENT: One 18in Mk IX torpedo

» **OCT 1916**
Sueter approaches Sopwith

» **JUN 1917**
Maiden flight of the prototype T.1

» **MAY 1918**
First Blackburn-built Cuckoo is delivered

» **OCT 2, 1918**
Cuckoo enters service with 185 Squadron

» **NOV 1918**
185 Sqn embarks on HMS *Argus*

» **APR 1, 1923**
Cuckoo retired by 210 Squadron

The First Landplane Designed for Carrier Ops

The single-seat Sopwith T.1 torpedo aircraft was the subject of a discussion between Sopwith and Commodore Murray Sueter of the Admiralty at the beginning of October 1916. The fact that Sopwith took with him drawings of the aircraft suggests, that the idea of a single-seat torpedo-carrying landplane originated at Kingston; it is, however, clear that the Admiralty tentatively suggested that either one or two torpedoes should be carried together with fuel for four hours' flying. Sopwith would have ruled out the two-torpedo capability in a single-engine aircraft small enough to be accommodated on any aircraft carrier likely to be planned in the foreseeable future. This discussion was confirmed in an Admiralty memorandum, dated October 9, requesting that the Sopwith Company should go ahead with the aircraft, expressing the view that some sort of catapult would be made available to assist the heavily-laden aircraft into the air.

The prototype T .1, which flew first in June 1917, was powered by a 200hp Hispano-Suiza engine and underwent official trials at the Isle of Grain the following month.The three-bay, unstaggered wings were made to fold on the plane of the inner pairs of interplane struts; these struts were constructed in halves along their length, the outboard halves being attached to the folding sections of the wings, and the inboard halves fixed so as to provide rigidity to wing structure. The undercarriage, attached to the fixed inboard wing section, comprised sturdy double-V struts.

The first production order for 100 Cuckoos was placed on August 16 with the Fairfield Shipbuilding & Engineering Company. Shortly afterwards Sir David Beatty put forward an ambitious plan for 200 Cuckoos to launch a torpedo offensive against the German Fleet in their harbours. Although this was not accepted as a realistic undertaking, an order was nevertheless placed for a further 50 Cuckoos with Pegler & Co Ltd of Doncaster.

Introducing the Cuckoo into production was beset with problems and delays. The Royal Aircraft Factory was given priority for deliveries of the Hispano-Suiza engine for its SE.5a, and as a result, the 200hp Sunbeam Arab was selected as an alternative; this change saw extensive alterations to the Cuckoo's nose structure, and the engine was further delayed by unsatisfactory performance and reliability during its development.

In February 1918, 230 further aircraft were ordered from the Blackburn Aeroplane & Motor Company, its first two Cuckoos being completed only two months later.

Fifty Blackburn-built Cuckoos had been completed by the end of August, and production was allowed to continue into 1919, by which time the company had built 162 aircraft in its factory at Sherburn-in-Elmet. Early production examples were delivered for pilot training at East Fortune, Scotland with the Torpedo Aeroplane School, and in October began to equip 185 Squadron, also at East Fortune. This squadron began to embark on HMS *Furious* on October 19, but did not take part in any combat operations before the Armistice, and was disbanded on April 14, 1919. In July 1919 Cuckoos joined 186 Squadron for naval co-operation duties at Gosport, remaining in service until April 1923.

An alternative to the Arab engine had been sought and a number of Cuckoos were fitted with the 275hp Wolseley W.4A Viper, and became known as the Cuckoo Mk II. Another aircraft, N7990, was flown experimentally with the 275hp Rolls-Royce Falcon III, but neither this nor the Viper gave any significant improvement in performance.

Once the Arab's early unreliability had been improved, the Cuckoo came to be generally liked by Service pilots, and its replacement by the Blackburn Dart from 1923 was more on account of a preference, then being expressed, for two-seat torpedo-bombers than any appreciable performance shortcoming in the Cuckoo.

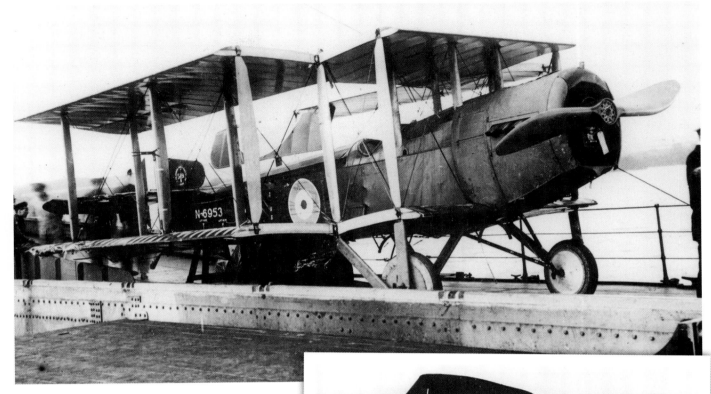

Above: The Cuckoo was a single-seat, three-bay, folding-wing torpedo-carrying biplane of wood and fabric construction designed by the Sopwith Aviation Co Ltd in 1916. It was powered by one 200hp Hispano-Suiza water-cooled engine.

Right: In service, the Cuckoo was generally popular with its pilots because the airframe was strong and the aircraft was easy to control.

Below: The Cuckoo was declared obsolete in April 1923, but six of the Viper-powered machines were taken to Japan in 1921 by the British Air Mission for the Imperial Japanese Navy.

As a potential replacement for the Bristol Fighter, the Bulldog was unleashed in mock combats against a 'Brisfit' and was found to be just about as manoeuvrable.

>> **MAR 1918**
Maiden flight of the Bulldog

>> **APR 22, 1918**
Official trials at Martlesham Heath

>> **MAR 1919**
Second prototype used for flight testing

Unsuccessful Brisfit Replacement

The Bulldog was designed as a two-seat fighter-reconnaissance aircraft with a view to possibly replacing the Bristol F.2B Fighter in RAF service. In its original form the compact aircraft first flew in 1917 with a 200hp Clerget 11Eb 11-cylinder rotary engine. The single-bay biplane was armed with two synchronised .303in machine guns and a further pair of .303s mounted in the rear cockpit. The Bulldog proved heavier than projected and difficult to control, and in an attempt to improve handling qualities it was fitted with two-bay wings with balanced ailerons, flight testing resuming in March 1918. With the balanced ailerons replaced by plain surfaces, the Bulldog was submitted to Martlesham Heath for official trials on April 22, 1918. There it was found to handle well, but possessed disappointing performance. It was eventually to be re-engined with a Bentley BR.2 The second prototype was completed with an ABC Dragonfly nine-cylinder radial of 320hp, being delivered to the RAE at

Farnborough on June 25, 1918 as the Bulldog Mk II and serving as an engine test bed. Work began on a third prototype, but the Bulldog's failure to win official approval led to discontinuation of the programme before this aircraft could be completed. The following data relates to the Clerget-engined Bulldog with two-bay wings and plain ailerons.

TECHNICAL DATA - BULLDOG

ENGINE: One 200hp Clerget 11Eb

WING SPAN: 33ft 9in

LENGTH: 23ft

HEIGHT: 8ft 9in

WING AREA: 335 sq/ft

EMPTY WEIGHT: 1,141lb

LOADED WEIGHT: 2,495lb

MAX SPEED: 109 mph at 10,000ft

SERVICE CEILING: 15,000ft

ENDURANCE: 2hrs

ARMAMENT: Two forward-firing .303in Vickers machine guns and two .303in Lewis machine guns in the rear cockpit

Among the Sopwith prototypes of 1918 was the Buffalo armoured two-seater for 'contact patrol' duties. As was the case with the Rhino and Hippo, the first example had a rocking-pillar mounting for the rear Lewis gun, whereas the second had a Scarff ring-mounting.

The Last Great War Sopwith

To dismiss the Buffalo, merely as a two-seat counterpart of the Salamander would be to understate its purpose and technical merits and to underrate its potential.

A trim, positively fighter-like appearance quite belied its poor performance; for any new warplane of 1918 having a maximum speed at low level of about 110 mph and a service ceiling of 9,000ft must be accounted poor indeed in this respect. And yet, when it is considered that the Buffalo's crew numbered two, each with a plentifully-fed machine-gun; that the engine was only 230hp; and that the weight of armour, though not precisely known, must in itself have been a formidable hindrance, then the figures seem far less distressful.

The Buffalo was, in fact, quite an object-lesson in design. In the first place, it was remarkably compact, for the two-bay wings spanned only about 3ft more than those of the single-seat Salamander or Snipe. Commensurately modest were the fuselage dimensions a fact to which the photographs attest by emphasising the relative bulk of the Bentley BR.2 engine and its associated fairings. The small cross-section behind the engine represented not merely economy in weight but a wide downward field of view for the gunner, while presenting a 'low profile' to return fire from the ground.

To Sopwith the Buffalo was known initially as a 'trench fighter' following the precedents of the special 'T.F.' Camel and the Salamander; but officially its purpose was 'contact patrol'. This specialised and dangerous function called for very low flying over the battle zone to determine by visual observation

or 'contact' the dispositions of the infantry; hence the protective armour. 'Offensive patrol' was a secondary consideration, implicit in the absence of bombing capability.

Clearly, a wide field of view for the pilot was a primary requirement, and this was met by seating him high, close behind the engine, with his head in a large, oblong centre-section cut-out. Very close behind him was the observer/gunner, whose upward view was enhanced by a trailing-edge cut-out, though whose downward vision was impeded - on the first machine especially - by the bottom wing.

Two Buffaloes, H5892 and H5893, were ordered in July 1918, the 'fighter' element in the design, already touched upon, being accentuated by the stipulation that as many Bulldog parts as possible should be embodied. This stipulation may well have been responsible in part for the speed with which H5892 was prepared for night-trials at Brooklands, where it arrived on September 18, 1918, and was photographed on the following day. On October 20, H5892 was flown to No.1 Aeroplane Supply Depot at Marquise, and experience in France brought recommended changes, though to what degree these were incorporated in H5893 when it was delivered to Martlesham Heath on November 18 is unsure. On both Buffaloes a prominent feature was the ring-sight for the pilot's gun, stayed by struts to the engine cowling, though there was provision also for a central Aldis sight.

Had the war not ended when it did there is little doubt that the Buffalo would have seen service in quantity.

TECHNICAL DATA
BUFFALO

ENGINE: One 230hp Bentley BR.2

WING SPAN: 36ft 6in

LENGTH: 23ft 3½in

HEIGHT: 9ft 6in

WING AREA: 326 sq/ft

EMPTY WEIGHT: 2,178lb

LOADED WEIGHT: 3,071lb

MAX SPEED: 114 mph at 1,000ft

SERVICE CEILING: 9,000ft

RANGE: 275 miles

ARMAMENT: One forward-firing .303in Vickers machine gun and one .303in Lewis machine gun in the rear cockpit

» **SEP 19, 1918**
Maiden flight of first prototype

» **OCT, 1918**
One Buffalo joins 4 Sqn AFC

» **DEC, 1918**
Both prototypes join 43 Sqn for evaluation

A counterpart of the D.H.9, the Rhino single-engined bomber of 1917 had internal bomb stowage. This was located under the pilot's seat, and the bombs, four 112lb or nine 50lb or twenty 20lb, were winched into place complete with release gear.

>> **OCT, 1917**
First prototype flies from Brooklands

>> **FEB, 1918**
Second prototype to Martlesham Heath

An Unimpressive Triplane Bomber

The Sopwith Rhino two-seat triplane bomber was a private venture, not intended to approximate to any official requirement, and therefore subject of a special licence (No 14) for the manufacture of two prototypes, X7 and X8. Designed during the late summer of 1917, the first aircraft was flown at Brooklands in October, powered by a 230hp BHP six-cylinder in-line water-cooled engine. The dominant feature, apart from the triplane wings, was the exceptionally deep fuselage, necessitated by the internal bomb bay beneath the pilot's cockpit, the bombs being loaded into a self-contained structure which was winched into the aircraft's bomb bay. The choice of the BHP engine, which was fully cowled, also resulted in a deep nose profile. The second Rhino was flown around the end of the year.

Although the engine was cooled by an orthodox water-circulation system, with radiators on the sides of the nose (each with an adjustable ramp shutter), a small frontal air intake was incorporated above the propeller shaft to provide additional cooling of the tandem cylinder blocks and exhaust manifold.

The single-bay wings, of generous area, were all fitted with ailerons and were rigged with slight stagger. The ailerons on both prototypes were originally horn-balanced, extending beyond the wing structure, but were later shortened to blend with the profile of the wing tips. The lower pairs of ailerons were interconnected by faired struts and the upper pairs by cables.

Front gun armament comprised a single synchronised Vickers gun above the nose decking, and rear protection was afforded by a Lewis gun on the rear cockpit; on X7 the rear gun was pillar-mounted, and on X8 a Scarff ring was provided. No bomb sight could be fitted, and downward view for the pilot (situated directly below the upper wing) was assisted by cut-out panels in the roots of the centre and lower wings.

The undercarriage comprised plain steel tubular V-struts with bungee-bound cross-axle, the whole wheel structure giving an impression of being understressed.

Both Rhinos were officially tested at Martlesham Heath in February and March 1918, but returned somewhat pedestrian performance figures with and without bomb load, and the aircraft was not accepted for production.

TECHNICAL DATA - RHINO

ENGINE: One 230hp B.H.P. (Beardmore Halford Pullinger)

WING SPAN: 33ft

LENGTH: 27ft 8in

HEIGHT: 10ft 11in

WING AREA: 545 sq/ft

EMPTY WEIGHT: 2,185lb

LOADED WEIGHT: 3,590lb

MAX SPEED: 114 mph at sea level

SERVICE CEILING: 12,000ft

ENDURANCE: 3hr 45min

ARMAMENT: One forward-firing .303in Vickers machine gun and one .303in Lewis machine gun in the rear cockpit and 450lb of bombs in a removable pack

In mid-1918 the Scooter was registered as K.135, then in mid-1919, as G-EACZ. Overhauled for C Clayton of Hendon a new CoA was dated August 1, 1925. In August 1926 it was sold to Dudley Watt, who used it frequently until, after it had flown in the Lympne Open Handicap of September 18, 1926, it was sold as scrap in 1927.

Unsuccessful Monoplane Camel Conversion

'If you want speed the monoplane has it' was the direct reason why these two little parasol machines were built. Harry Hawker's was the name most closely linked with 'Sopwith Monoplane No.1', as the Scooter was first known; for not only did he use it as a runabout after its completion in July 1918, but it was he who bought it in April 1921. By that time it had been registered to the Sopwith Company, first as K.135, then in mid-1919, as G-EACZ.

The Scooter's fuselage was that of a standard 130hp Clerget-powered F.1 Camel; nor did the tail differ noticeably. The swept-back monoplane wing, however, was altogether new. It was mounted very close to the fuselage on short splayed-out struts, and with a tall pyramidal cabane above these struts to anchor four landing wires which ran from its apex to the wing upper surfaces on each side. Below the wing, running up from the bottom longerons, were corresponding flying wires. So close was the wing to the fuselage that a trailing-edge cut-out was a necessity rather than a convenience.

Although the Swallow greatly resembled the Scooter it was, in fact, considerably different, having, in the first place, a wing of greater span and larger area a fact that might be related to the joint demands of shipboard operation and the fitting of armament. Even so, the area was much less, figures being 162 sq/ft and 221 sq/ft and this figure for the Camel was appreciably less than that for the corresponding land-based version. Stiffness was augmented by multiple chordwise external strips between the spars - to a greater extent than on the Buffalo biplane; the wing was higher set above the fuselage than on the Scooter, necessitating longer attachment struts beneath the landing-wire pylon; and partly by reason of a new wingtip shape, but also because of their greater span - the ailerons were increased in area.

While the raised mounting of the parasol wing may in some measure have been dictated by considerations of pilot-view, this feature also allowed easier installation of, and access to, the two synchronised Vickers guns that formed the armament. These guns were more widely spaced than on the similarly armed Camel and lay almost wholly exposed - certainly lacking the familiar 'hump' with combined large ejection chutes for cases and links immediately below them. Ring-and-bead sights were fitted for Martlesham Heath trials.

Apart from the gun installation and cowling, the Swallow's fuselage adhered closely to standard Camel F.1 practice. Indeed, the Swallow which was sometimes called 'Monoplane No. 2' still bore the number B9276, proclaiming its Boulton & Paul origins as one of a Camel F.1 batch.

The Swallow was tested with a 110hp Le Rhone, but in round figures results showed that it would have still been 5mph slower than a similarly powered Camel. The aircraft was developed too late for the Great War and thus did not enter production.

TECHNICAL DATA SWALLOW

ENGINE: One 110hp le Rhône 9J

WING SPAN: 28ft 10in

LENGTH: 18ft 9in

HEIGHT: 10ft 2in

WING AREA: 160 sq/ft

EMPTY WEIGHT: 889lb

LOADED WEIGHT: 1,420lb

MAX SPEED: 113.5 mph at 10,000ft

SERVICE CEILING: 18,500ft

ARMAMENT: Two forward-firing .303in Vickers machine guns

» **JUL 1918**
Maiden flight of the Scooter

» **OCT 28, 1918**
Swallow delivered to Martlesham Heath

» **1927**
Scooter is scrapped

Of all the names applied to Sopwith aircraft, the Snail was by far the most appropriate, not in the sense that the aeroplane which bore it was slow, but because it had a shell-type, or monocoque, fuselage.

>> **APR, 1918**
First prototype Snail is completed

>> **MAY 9, 1918**
Snail delivered to Martlesham Heath

>> **OCT 1918**
Wasp engine abandoned

Underpowered and Under-Performing

In October 1917, the A.B.C. Wasp seven-cylinder radial air-cooled engine was considered to offer much promise, and on the 31st of that month Sopwith was invited by the Air Board to tender designs for a single-seat fighter utilising that power plant. Four prototypes were ordered, these being of conventional construction, and, on November 23, the company was asked to build two additional prototypes with plywood monocoque fuselages. In view of its intended function, the adoption of the name Snail for the new single-seater was bizarre, this being approved on February 16, 1918. Powered by a 170hp Wasp I, the first prototype Snail was completed in April 1918, this having negative wing stagger and fabric skinning for its circular-section fuselage. Intended armament comprised two synchronised 0.303in machine guns, a third weapon of similar calibre being mounted above the wing centre section, to starboard of the cut-out. The remaining three prototypes of conventional construction were not completed, the next Snail to fly being the first of the two with plywood monocoque fuselages and positive

wing stagger. On May 9, the monocoque Snail was sent to Martlesham Heath for official trials, the reports being less than complimentary about its manoeuvrability and low-speed control. When, in October 1918, it was decided to abandon the Wasp engine, further work on the Snail was terminated, the second monocoque prototype being discontinued before completion.

TECHNICAL DATA - SNAIL

ENGINE: One 170hp ABC Wasp

WING SPAN: 25ft 4in

LENGTH: 19ft

HEIGHT: 7ft 10in

WING AREA: 250 sq/ft

EMPTY WEIGHT: 1,390lb

LOADED WEIGHT: 1,920lb

MAX SPEED: 124.5 mph at 10,000ft

CLIMB RATE: 9min 55sec to 10,000ft

ARMAMENT: Two forward-firing .303in Vickers machine guns and Lewis above the upper wing

Designed in parallel with the Snark triplane and similarly intended to meet the requirements of the RAF's Type I specification, the Snapper single-bay staggered equi-span biplane was destined to be the last fighter to bear the Sopwith name before the company went into liquidation in September 1920.

Snipe Replacement with Engine Woes

'The machine is, we believe, known as the Sopwith Snapper', coyly ventured *Flight* in commenting on the single-seat biplane, wearing racing number 17, that was to have been flown by Harry Hawker in the 1919 Aerial Derby.

The magazine continued: 'It can now be asserted that this aircraft was a Snapper; that the engine was a 320hp ABC Dragonfly I radial; that although the aircraft bore the registration K-149 on the fuselage side-panels it was later allotted the letters G-EAFJ; that this particular Snapper was seemingly one of three that had been designed to the RAF Type I specification; and that all three of these were at the RAE, Farnborough, as late as June 1920.

'Aerodynamically and structurally the type had inter-related features of special interest, notably that, although having a single-bay wing cellule, this structure was uncommon in embodying a broad-span top centre section that was strut-braced well inboard of the attachment points for the outer panels, and also in having the single set of interplane struts placed far outboard. The result was to emphasise that the Snapper was no mere biplane version of the Snark for the Snark's top centre-section struts were splayed out to the main attachment points. Simply stated, it looked as though the Snapper was asking to become a 1½ Strutter once again.'

The wings were relatively broad in chord and the moderate aspect ratio gave a lower service ceiling than was attainable by the Dragon or the Dolphin Mk II. Nevertheless, this very feature of broad chord accentuated the Snapper's trim appearance, though this was somewhat marred

because the two staggered Vickers guns were largely exposed by reason of the small cross-section of the fuselage. Had a Snark-type monocoque fuselage been used, as was at first intended, the guns might have been enclosed, with advantage to appearance and performance. As things turned out, the Snapper bore a striking resemblance to the Pup and so Sopwith fighter design appeared in the Snapper to have turned almost full circle.

Although three examples, numbered F7031-F7033, were ordered early in 1918, and by May/June work on the first was well advanced, it was at one stage intended to reduce the order to one, with an ordinary wire-braced wooden fabric-covered fuselage. In the event, all three Snappers were completed the first of these, F7031, appearing at Brooklands in April 1919. In June, the civil-registered K-149 made its debut. The RAF identity of this machine if any is indeterminate, and the fact that K-149 was unarmed, and faired accordingly, has scant significance. It could well have been F7031 in a new guise, as indeed could the Snapper that was tested at Martlesham Heath in September 1919. The most obvious modification on this last-mentioned version, however, was a much-revised installation of the Dragonfly engine. In this instance the nose fairing was of such proportions that it could no longer be termed a crankcase-cowling, leaving, as it did, much less of each cylinder exposed to cooling air. It was fronted, moreover, by a very large blunt-nosed open-centred spinner, which left the front flange of the propeller hub exposed.

TECHNICAL DATA
SNAPPER

ENGINE: One 360hp ABC Dragonfly

WING SPAN: 28ft

LENGTH: 20ft 7in

HEIGHT: 10ft

WING AREA: 292 sq/ft

EMPTY WEIGHT: 1,462lb

LOADED WEIGHT: 2,190lb

MAX SPEED: 140 mph at 10,000ft

SERVICE CEILING: 23,000ft

CLIMB RATE: 7min 50sec to 10,000ft

ARMAMENT: Two forward-firing .303in Vickers machine guns

» **JUN 6, 1918**
Three Snapper prototypes ordered

» **AUG 1919**
Snapper delivered to Martlesham Heath

» **JUN 1920**
All three prototypes at Farnborough

Despite the fact that, by 1918, the triplane configuration was widely considered as passé for the fighter, on May 14 of that year, Sopwith was awarded a contract for three prototypes of a new single-seat fighting triplane, conforming to the RAF Type I specification and named the Snark.

» **OCT 1918**
First prototype completed

» **JUL 1919**
Maiden flight of first prototype

» **1921**
Last example grounded

TECHNICAL DATA SNARK

ENGINE: One 360hp ABC Dragonfly IA

WING SPAN: 26ft 6in

LENGTH: 20ft 6in

HEIGHT: 10ft 10in

WING AREA: 322 sq/ft

LOADED WEIGHT: 2,283lb

MAX SPEED: 130 mph at 3,000ft

ARMAMENT: Two forward-firing .303in Vickers machine guns and four .303in Lewis under the wings

Wooden Monocoque Triplane Fighter

In respect of airframe and armament, the Snark was one of Sopwith's most remarkable creations and only in fairly recent times has its full significance been recognised.

Reversion to the triplane formula was interesting from several aspects, notably in that the Snark was designed to meet the same general requirements - those of the RAF Type I specification - as the similarly powered Snapper biplane, described in the following chapter. The generous wing area afforded by this formula, 322 sq/ft against the 292 sq/ft of the Snapper - was considered to be beneficial both to performance and handling at altitude (especially when two Vickers guns were the sole armament) or, alternatively, to the carrying of a greatly increased armament, though obviously, in this case, with some sacrifice in performance generally. The maximum speed was, in fact, at least 10 mph less than the Snapper's.

The wing arrangement was far more complex than that of the famous rotary - engined Triplane single-seater of 1916, for not only were the interplane struts of 'normal', that is, double-form, but stagger was sharply unequal. As formerly, there were ailerons on all six main wing panels.

Of even greater interest perhaps was the monocoque fuselage, with the basic armament of two Vickers guns almost literally built-in to it, slightly below the centre line and almost at the level of the rudder bar. The rounded cross-section of the fuselage blended very happily with the installation of the ABC Dragonfly radial engine, whether a spinner was fitted or not.

Three Snarks (F4068-F4070) were ordered in April 1918, and by June 26 the still-uncovered wings of F4068 had been attached to the fuselage. The Vickers guns had been installed during May. Nevertheless, it was decided in October that only this first example of the Snark should be finished and delivered - a decision which was not, in the event, acted upon. By October the airframe of F4068 had already been cleared for flight though an acceptable engine was not delivered until December. Peacetime-pace and magneto trouble apparently shared the blame for the installation not being completed until April 1919. In July there was an engine-change, and trials did not take place until September. By the end of 1919, Snarks F4069 and F4070 had been completed, and on November 12, F4068 was delivered to Martlesham Heath, though it was soon returned to Sopwith for another engine-change before resuming its official trials at Martlesham in March 1920.

Concerning the second Snark, F4069, little is known, though F4070 ultimately flew early in 1921. As tested at Martlesham Heath F4070 had a very large spinner, a modified engine cowling and very prominent air intakes for the carburettors, these intakes extending downwards from behind the engine almost half-way to the axle. The vertical tail-surfaces appear to have been identical with those of F4068; thus the side area of the new engine installation could have been of little consequence in this connection, and 'the hunting of the Snark' may not have become a serious phenomenon.

The Gnu was designed to meet the requirements of a light, high-speed machine for passengers or cargo. It was equipped either with the 200hp Bentley rotary or with the 110hp Le Rhône.

One of the Earliest Civilian Cabin Aircraft

In several respects the Gnu was the most interesting and promising of the three civilian offerings that were introduced by Sopwith to the public around mid-1919. As early as May 29, 1919, the first Gnu (K-101) was flown by Harry Hawker to Hendon, the occasion being the subsequent reception accorded to the US Navy-Curtiss flying-boat crewmen who had just completed the first Atlantic crossing by air, by way of the Azores and Lisbon.

Sopwith's re-entry into the civil passenger-carrying business was marked with due ceremony and a sense of public relations, no less than 60 guineas being paid by Miss Daisy King of Leeds, not so much for the privilege of trying the new aeroplane as being flown by the heroic Hawker!

Two passengers were seated side by side under a glazed roof which hinged outwards from the centre in two sections, though from K-140 onwards most of the Gnus dispensed with this elaboration, and the passenger compartment was open. That the hinged roof was in any case a concession to post-war 'refinement' rather than actual demand may have been implicit in The Aeroplane's remark that the Gnu should appeal to those who desired 'to travel by air in comfort, relative silence, and the absence of wind' quite as strongly as would the Dove to those 'who rather prefer to experience even the minor discomforts of flying rather than forgo any of its sensations.'

Most of the Gnu fleet were used to provide joyrides in the UK in the early 1920s but two examples were sent to Australia - including this example sponsored by Witch Soap. The Australian examples were mostly used by Australian Aerial Services to provide a mail service between Adelaide and Sydney.

>> **1919**
Gnu introduced to the public

>> **MAY 29, 1919**
K-101 flown by Harry Hawker to Hendon

>> **JUN 23, 1923**
G-EAGP wins the Grosvenor Challenge Cup

TECHNICAL DATA - GNU

ENGINE: One 110hp le Rhône	**MAX SPEED:** 93 mph
WING SPAN: 38ft 1in	**CLIMB RATE:** 645 ft/min
LENGTH: 25ft 10in	**RANGE:** 300 miles
HEIGHT: 9ft 10in	**ACCOMMODATION:** One pilot and
LOADED WEIGHT: 3,350lb	two passengers

The Sopwith Schneider Seaplane, G-EAKI, taking off in front of Bournemouth pier in September 1919.

» SEP 10, 1919
Schneider Trophy at Bournemouth

» 1920
Aircraft rebuilt as a landplane

» 1922
Rainbow rebuilt by Hawker Engineering

» AUG 6, 1923
Rainbow finishes 2nd in Aerial Derby

» SEP 1, 1923
Rainbow destroyed in crash

TECHNICAL DATA SCHNEIDER SEAPLANE

ENGINE: One 450hp Cosmos Jupiter

WING SPAN: 24ft

LENGTH: 21ft 6in

HEIGHT: 10ft

WING AREA: 221¾ sq/ft

GROSS WEIGHT: 2,200lb

MAX SPEED: 170 mph

Post-War Schneider Contender

The Schneider Trophy contest at Bournemouth in September 1919 was an opportunity to show the world how British aircraft-designers and constructors had progressed, and how advantage could be taken of the latest aero-engines.

Though France and Italy were both well represented, it will suffice here to record that the British entries were a short-span Fairey III, Supermarine Sea Lion I, Avro 539A and a superb Sopwith creation. The latter was a Cosmos Jupiter-powered floatplane dubbed – unsurprisingly – the Sopwith Schneider Cup Racer.

The powerful Jupiter would find fame when it was produced under licence by Bristol for its Bulldog fighter.

In the Sopwith racer (which was registered G-EAKI) the Jupiter's nine cylinders were faired in with cone-shaped streamlining and the aircraft's four fuel tanks were similarly streamlined into the circular cross-sectioned fuselage. The fuselage itself was of the usual wooden cross-braced construction but covered by a mixture of aluminium and fabric. Bracing of the stubby single-bay wings was by streamline wires, and there were ailerons on all four panels.

On the day of the race the weather was poor, with thick fog causing pilot Harry Hawker to abandon the race. The Fairey entry also withdrew and the Supermarine Sea Lion hit debris while the pilot was landing to see where he was on the course. The only aircraft to complete the race, the Italian SIAI S.13 was disqualified as the pilot consistently some one of the

> ❝ **ON THE DAY OF THE RACE THE WEATHER WAS POOR, WITH THICK FOG CAUSING PILOT HARRY HAWKER TO ABANDON THE RACE.** ❞

turning points and the race was declared void.

In 1920, the Schneider Cup racer was rebuilt as a landplane and re-engined with a neatly cowled 320hp ABC Dragonfly as the Jupiter engine which powered it in 1919 was unavailable. This engine has a cubic capacity that was roughly 25% smaller than the Jupiter.

The new aircraft was renamed as the Sopwith Rainbow and was entered into the 1920 Aerial Derby with the Race Number 13. Perhaps this was to an open as although the aeroplane performed well it was disqualified from the race after the Sopwith Company's liquidation on September 11, 1920. Harry Hawker had also planned to race the aeroplane in the 1920 Gordon Bennett Aviation Cup race in France but was forced to withdraw from the field.

However, this was not the end of the Rainbow, even if no pot of gold awaited it. With a Jupiter installed once again, the airframe was refurbished and the legend 'Sopwith Hawker' painted on the fin so as to follow its elegant contour. In this format G-EAKI not only appeared at Croydon for the 1923 Aerial Derby held on August Bank Holiday, but finished second - to Larry Carter in the Gloster I.

The pilot was Walter Longton, and his speed was 164.02mph. Although it had been planned to refit floats and to try once again for the Schneider Trophy, the spinner of the Rainbow came adrift while Longton was making a final test of the aircraft as a landplane on September 1. Longton was lucky to emerge unharmed from the forced-landing near Brooklands and the Rainbow never flew again.

The Sopwith Schneider G-EAKI, which retired during the 1919 Schneider Trophy contest owing to fog over the course.

With the legend 'Sopwith Hawker' painted on the fin, G-EAKI is pictured at Croydon for the 1923 Aerial Derby (the last of the series) held on August Bank Holiday.

The Sopwith Rainbow; a re-engined, renamed and reduced-span landplane version of G-EAKI – 'reduced' denoting that the span was shorter by 3 ft.

Sopwith designer George Carter based his design for the Transatlantic (Atlantic) on the single-engined Sopwith B.1 bomber.

The Race Across the Atlantic – *Flight* article (April 10, 1919)

» **MAR 28, 1919**
Atlantic despatched to Newfoundland

» **MAY 18, 1919**
Hawker and Grieves' take off from St Johns

TECHNICAL DATA ATLANTIC

ENGINE: One 375hp Rolls Royce Eagle VIII
WING SPAN: 46ft 6in
LENGTH: 32ft
HEIGHT: 11ft
WING AREA: 575 sq/ft
EMPTY WEIGHT: 3,000lb
LOADED WEIGHT: 6,150lb
MAX SPEED: 118 mph
SERVICE CEILING: 13,000ft

'The preparations for the great race to be first to cross the Atlantic by air are progressing apace. By way of summary, the Sopwith machine, to be piloted by Harry Hawker, who will have with him as navigator and assistant pilot Capt Grieve, is already at the starting point in Newfoundland, and is only awaiting favourable weather conditions before making a start. The Martinsyde biplane, with its pilot, F P Raynham, and his navigator, Capt Morgan, is on its way across, and may, by the time these lines appear in print, have arrived at St John's. The Fairey machine, up till now the only seaplane entered from this side, is rapidly nearing completion, being, in fact, a standard Fairey 3C type especially adapted for the race. The Short machine entered, and which will be piloted by Mjr Wood, who will have with him as navigator Capt Wyllie, has the distinction of being the only entrant which, so far, it is proposed to start from this side, the starting point chosen being Bawnmore, near Limerick, in Ireland. This machine, which has been undergoing severe tests during the last couple of weeks, is to be flown first to Ireland, whence the final start will be made.

'As to the probability of one or all of the competitors succeeding in getting across, there is of course, a certain element of luck involved, but arrangements, as announced elsewhere, are being made., by the Air Ministry and Admiralty, to take all possible precautions, and to ensure that, even in cases of engine failure, the occupants should have a very good chance of being picked up by passing vessels.

'The Rolls-Royce engined Sopwith transport type specially designed for an attempt to win the *Daily Mail* Prize for crossing the Atlantic, is of the vertical biplane type, the wings having no stagger. Pilot and navigator are seated well aft, so as to give a large space in the fuselage between them and the engine, in which to fit the large petrol tank required for the great amount of

fuel that has to be carried for a flight of this duration. This tank has a capacity of 330 gallons, while the oil tank contains 24 gallons, and the water reservoir 17 gallons. The weight of the machine empty is 3,000lbs, and fully loaded she weighs 6,150lbs. The engine fitted is a 375hp Rolls-Royce Eagle, which will give the machine a maximum speed of 118 mph. This speed will not, of course, be maintained all the way, the most economical speed from the point of fuel consumption lying somewhere between the maximum and the minimum speed, and varying with the lightening in load as the fuel is consumed.

'The cockpit of the occupants is arranged in a somewhat unusual way, the two seats being side by side, but somewhat staggered in relation to one another. The object of this seating arrangement is to enable them to communicate with one another more readily and to facilitate 'changing watches' during the long journey. The very deep turtle back of the fuselage is made in part detachable, the portion which is strapped on being built so as to form a small life boat in case of a forced descent on the sea. In this manner it is hoped to provide sufficient flotation for the occupants to remain afloat until a passing vessel may pick them up, should a descent be necessary. As the machine is not fitted with floats, it would, of course, be out of the question to get her off again once she was in the water. In other respects the machine does not differ greatly from standard Sopwith practice, which is already well known to readers of Flight.'

Hawker and Grieves finally took off from St John's on 18 May 1919. During the night, however, the aircraft's engine started to overheat. With heavy weather ahead, they turned south to seek out the shipping lanes, and on encountering the Danish steamer SS *Mary* ditched in the Atlantic and were rescued.

The Antelope with its original ailerons, but with its four-wheeled landing gear. The cabin door was a notable feature, and its handle shows clearly.

Award Winning Three-Seat Transport

The Antelope was quite a notable aeroplane in the development of civil flying as, indeed, it had to be to gain the second prize in the Air Ministry Small Commercial Aeroplane Competition in 1920.

The one-and-only Antelope was built by Sopwith in 1919, with a normal V-strut landing gear. In 1920, Sopwith described it in these terms: 'The Antelope is intended to serve the purpose of a utility machine, characterised by the highest possible performance compatible with great structural strength and having a wide speed range of 38 to 100 mph. Accommodation is provided for pilot and two passengers, the former being located high up between the main planes, whilst the latter are enclosed in a comfortable cabin of 50 cu/ft capacity, aft of the planes. A door in the side of the cabin enables the passengers to enter straight from the ground. Triplex windows in the cabin provide a good field of view, whilst one of the passenger's seats is adjustable so that, on sliding open a door in the roof, the passenger may sit in the open if desired. The engine, an 180hp Hispano-Suiza Viper, is enclosed by a quickly detachable cowling, giving extreme accessibility, and is fitted with a Black and Manson self-starter, operated from the pilot's cockpit. A fireproof bulkhead is interposed between the fuel tanks and engine. There are no welded joints in the machine. A pair of front wheels which will protect the propeller and prevent the machine from nosing over on landing. A steel tube steerable tail skid is provided, and the opening in the floor of the body through which the skid passes has a flexible cover of oilcloth which prevents dirt thrown up by the skid from getting inside the fuselage.'

The adjustable seat mentioned was the rear one, and the occupant was raised by sitting on the hinged back-rest which could be folded forwards on to the arm-rests of the wicker seat. The passenger's head then protruded through an apparently conventional cockpit opening, with vee-shaped windscreen, the so-called 'door' in the roof being, more descriptively, a panel, shaped to the turtle-decking of the fuselage and sliding in side-channels running forward of the opening.

Certainly the Antelope made a good impression when shown at Olympia in July 1920, and a little later in that year its technical merits were more openly manifest when, with a new landing gear and ailerons reduced in chord by being tapered inwards, it participated in the Air Ministry Small Commercial Aeroplane Competition conducted at Martlesham Heath. The engine was then declared as a 200hp Wolseley Hispano Viper.

During the course of the Martlesham competitions Hawker came gliding in with brakes already applied, thus bursting both main tyres and one of the smaller forward ones. In any case, this stopped the Antelope within the stipulated distance, though this unmatched achievement failed to secure official recognition as the aeroplane was not intact. Nevertheless, the Antelope was awarded the second prize of £3,000. The winner was the Westland Limousine.

Yet this was not the Antelope's finish, for with F P Raynham as pilot it won the Surrey Open Handicap Race at Croydon in June 1922, and re-engined with a Siddeley Puma and re-registered as G-AUSS was transferred by the makers to the Larkin-Sopwith Aviation Company in Australia during April 1923. This company later became the Larkin Aircraft Supply Co. Ltd, and went into liquidation in 1934.

TECHNICAL DATA ANTELOPE

ENGINE: One 180hp Wolseley Viper

WING SPAN: 46ft 6in

LENGTH: 31ft

HEIGHT: 11ft 3in

WING AREA: 550 sq/ft

EMPTY WEIGHT: 2,387lb

LOADED WEIGHT: 3,450lb

MAX SPEED: 110 mph

CLIMB RATE: 5,000ft in 7mins 30sec

ENDURANCE: 4hrs

ACCOMMODATION: One pilot and two passengers

» **1920**
Aircraft on display at Olympia Aero Show

» **AUG 10, 1920**
Antelope issued with CoA

» **1935**
Aircraft still extant in Australia

As its name suggested, the Wallaby had very strong Australian associations, for it was built at Kingston-on-Thames under the personal supervision of an Australian (Harry Hawker) to compete for the £10,000 prize which had been offered by the Australian Government in March 1919.

›› OCT 21, 1919
Wallaby G-EAKS leaves Hounslow

›› APR 17, 1920
Aircraft crashes on Bali

TECHNICAL DATA WALLABY

ENGINE: One 375hp Rolls Royce Eagle VIII

WING SPAN: 46ft 6in

LENGTH: 31ft 6in

EMPTY WEIGHT: 2,780lb

GROSS WEIGHT: 5,200lb

MAX SPEED: 115 mph

CRUISING SPEED: 107 mph

ACCOMMODATION: Two crew and later converted to carry eight passengers

England to Australia Long-Range Biplane

The Wallaby was designed to compete in an Australian government £10,000 prize for an England to Australia flight. The following contemporary account of the Wallaby is of particular interest:

'It is a three-strutter machine, with a slight dihedral, of somewhere about the same size as the Transatlantic machine, to which, of course, it bears much resemblance. It is, however, a good deal more lightly loaded than its predecessor, as it only carries 200 gals, of petrol instead of 350. The actual machine is slightly heavier and stronger in construction. The arrangement of the cockpit has several features of special interest. The pilot's seat can be raised so that he looks out over the top of the fuselage or lowered and a lid pulled down over his head so that the occupants are entirely enclosed. There are two rudder bars at different heights. The passenger's seat can similarly be moved, and there is a complete set of dual controls, the joy sticks being removable. The whole place is quite roomy, and has windows of triplex glass. Capt Matthews finds he can see perfectly well from inside the fuselage, which has a window below as well as at the sides. There is an air intake to bring fresh air to the occupants instead of air tainted with engine oil, and windows at the side can be opened. It is, of course, well fitted out with instruments; besides the usual engine one, the compasses, and the airspeed meter, there is a turn-meter, which by recording the difference of air pressure on the two wing tips, tells the pilot if he is keeping on a straight course when he is in a mist; there is a flow meter, recording the rate of consumption of petrol, which works out at about 15 gals, an hour; a spirit-level for sideways motion, and an inclinometer for measuring the angle fore and aft; and an azimuth mirror for checking the compass by readings from the heavenly bodies on a system patented by Capt Matthews himself. The window below the pilot too is marked in degrees so that he can observe the direction of drift. There is a wheel at the side for altering the angle of the empennage in flight. The modern pilot, especially if he is also the navigator, has plenty to attend to.'

Clearly, this last remark was true - especially on its arduous expedition; and after setting out from Hounslow on October 21, 1919, Matthews and Kay clearly deserved the success that was nevertheless denied them by bad weather, one arrest, and damage in Persia. Eventually they crashed when landing in Bali, in the Netherlands East Indies, on April 17, 1920.

This chapter of accidents was not the Wallaby's end however, for it was shipped on to Australia, rebuilt as an eight-seater, and its registration changed to G-AUDU, on behalf of Australian Aerial Services Ltd.

The Sopwith Grasshopper, a conventional two-seat open cockpit biplane which was powered by a 100hp Anzani engine.

Two-Seat Tourer

The Sopwith Grasshopper was a one-off two-seat touring biplane built in 1920 and registered G-EAIN.

Although it was clearly not a success in the post-war civil market, it had its points of interest. Very apparent among these was its extremely low full-load landing speed of 35mph; indeed, its suitability for small-field operation, together with its physical appearance, may well have suggested its whimsical name.

Although only one example was built the Grasshopper enjoyed a popular following for nine years with five different owners. It was originally delivered in December 1922 to L C G M Le Champion but in May 1923 it transferred to E A D Eldridge. In February 1925 G-EAIN was sold to John Cobb but by August it was passed to Dudley Watt. Finally, Miss C R Leathart acquired it in February 1928 and she flew it until the Certificate of Airworthiness expired in May 1929. By this time the green-painted Grasshopper had afforded many people great joy, not least when flown round Brooklands motor-racing track on joyriding duties in 1926. It was not unheard of for

pilot J King to fly under the Byfleet bridge with passengers aboard – so this was clearly a gentle, if inelegant, aeroplane.

Part of its charm lay in the fact that Sopwith had chosen to fit an Anzani radial engines whereas the contemporary and comparable Avro 504K family was mostly fitted with rotary powerplants.

By this time Anzani engines were already historic as well as being very technically advanced. Its rotary powerplants were simple, light and compact and had seen extensive use during the Great War.

Yet once the war was over, prospective aircraft-owners (many of whom had been wartime pilots) wanted to leave behind them the concomitant associations of high consumption figures (both in petrol and oil), the inevitable gyroscopic effect produced by an entire engine that spun together with the propeller and an inseparable grimy, clammy feeling of spilled oil. Thus, in the post-war light-aircraft field, the Sopwith Grasshopper helped to stake a very firm claim indeed for the radial engine.

> **" CLEARLY, THIS AEROPLANE WAS A GENTLE, IF INELEGANT, CREATION "**

TECHNICAL DATA GRASSHOPPER

ENGINE: One 100hp Anzani 10

WING SPAN: 33ft 1in

LENGTH: 23ft 1in

HEIGHT: 9ft

GROSS WEIGHT: 1,670lb

MAX SPEED: 90 mph

ACCOMMODATION: One pilot and one passenger

» **MAR 22, 1920**
CoA issued to the Grasshopper

» **MAY 1929**
CoA expired

SOPWITH SURVIVORS

Of the many thousands of aircraft manufactured by the Sopwith Aircraft Company between 1912 and 1920 just over 20 original examples survive into the 21st Century. These are joined by a variety of replicas, of varying scale and accuracy, as the assorted models mark their 100th anniversaries.

Of all the Sopwith designs it is the Camel that has survived in the largest number – with eight original airframes in existence, albeit the majority of them as static museum exhibits.

Perhaps the most famous of the Camels on display is the RAF Museum's example, F6314. Built by Boulton & Paul as an F.1 variant in July 1918 the aircraft was placed into storage in 1919 and purchased by retired RFC Camel pilot Grenville O'Manton in 1923 as an engineless airframe.

The pilot fitted a lower powered radial engine in place of the original rotary (believed to be in an attempt to make it a more docile flying machine) but it only flew twice as it was so underpowered. It then passed through various owners before Richard Nash acquired it in 1936.

In 1939 the Camel went on display at the Science Museum in London but it was stored throughout the war years and eventually joined the RAF Museum on loan. It was eventually acquired for the museum in 1992 and is now on display at Hendon, suspended from the ceiling of the former Grahame White Factory.

The Imperial War Museum's Camel 2F.1 (N6812) is on display at its Lambeth facility in central London. N6812 was a 'Ship's Camel', featuring a shorter wingspan and a pair of Lewis guns above the wings. This was the aircraft that Flt Sub Lt Stuart Culley was flying on August 11, 1918 when he shot down Zeppelin *LZ100*, the last airship kill of the war. He did this after taking off from a tiny flight deck being towed behind a naval destroyer and climbing to 18,000ft. Culley then returned to the ship and ditched alongside it before both he and Camel were winched to safety. The aircraft was saved for posterity and has been on display at Lambeth since 1935.

▲ The Vintage Aviator Ltd operates an extensive collection of original, new-build and replica Great War aircraft. These include this pair of highly accurate replica Sopwiths – with Pup 'N6205' leading Camel 'B3889.' The latter features a number of original components, including a 160hp Gnome rotary engine. *TVAL/Gavin Conroy*

International Camels

Further afield, Camel B7280 is on display at the Polish Aviation Museum in Krakow and B5747 can be seen at the Royal Army and Military History Museum in Brussels – the latter wearing Belgian markings.

B7280 was the last of a batch of 100 Camels built by Clayton and Shuttleworth and was powered by a 150hp Bentley BR.1. It was the aircraft flown by RFC Lt H A Patey (who shot down nine German aircraft while flying this Camel) and Flying Officer J H Foreman. The latter also flew B7280 in combat, claiming two German machines before he was forced to land behind enemy lines. The camel was captured and was put on display in Berlin until the start of World War Two when it was moved to Poland for safekeeping. The remains were later passed to the Polish Aviation Museum and in the late 2000s it was restored. With eleven 'kills' to its name B7280 is one of the most notable survivors of the Great War.

Many Canadians flew the Camel but the only example preserved in the nation is Camel 2F.1 N8156, which is on display at the Canada Aviation and Space Museum in Ottawa, Ontario. This airframe was built too late to see service during the Great War but served the RAF until 1925 when it was one of six transferred to the Royal Canadian Air Force. It was later restored to fly in 1966 but was retired and presented to the museum a year later.

The only example of the Camel on static

▲ The Imperial War Museum's Camel 2F.1 (N6812) is currently suspended within its Lambeth facility in central London. This is the aircraft that Flt Sub Lt Stuart Culley was flying on August 11, 1918 when he shot down Zeppelin *LZ100*, the last airship kill of the war.

display in the USA is C8228, which is exhibited at the National Naval Aviation Museum in Pensacola, Florida, but one of the rare airworthy survivors is also based 'state-side.' B6291, owned by the Javier Arango Collection in California, was built at Kingston-on-Thames in 1917 and was sent to France where it flew with 10 Naval Squadron. It was substantially wrecked twice in flying accidents and the remains were acquired post-war by two pilots who intended to restore it. The plan never materialised and the Camel was found in a barn near Lincoln in the early 1980s. Restored as G-ASOP for AJD Engineering it flew again in July 1993 and was based at Old Warden for a year before it was sold to the USA.

The only other flyer in the world is ZK-SDL, which flies with The Vintage Aviator Ltd (TVAL) in

▲ The RAF Museum's Camel (F6314) is hoisted into position in the ceiling of the Graham White hangar at Hendon. *RAFM*

Among the many replica Camels in museums around the world is 'F6034' - an example built to original drawings for the National Museum of the United States Air Force in Dayton, Ohio. It is marked as the Camel flown by Lt George A Vaughn Jr while flying with the 17th Aero Squadron. *USAF Museum*

New Zealand. The airframe was shipped to the USA in 1920 and is believed to be N6254, but its data-plate was stolen while on display in Atlantic City so its exact identity is uncertain.

The airframe was stored during Second World War Two before being sold to Frank Tallman in 1950. Tallman restored the Camel to fly as part of his aerial filming fleet but it was eventually sold to the National Air and Space Museum and then the Aerospace Education Center in Little Rock, Arkansas. The latter closed in 2011 and the Camel was sold to TVAL in 2015. It has since been restored to flight.

TVAL also operated the very accurate reproduction Camel ZK-JMU. This aircraft was originally built in the USA by Gerry Thornhill and Carl Swanson and features a number of original components, including a 160hp Gnome rotary engine. The aircraft was exported to New Zealand in 1998 and in 2001 film producer Peter Jackson acquired it. Today it flies as 'B3889', the aircraft flown by Clive Collett with 70 Sqn.

Other flyable Camel replicas include the newly created Northern Aircraft Workshops example (G-BZSC) at the Shuttleworth Collection [see page 56] and Personal Plane Services' radial powered G-BPOB. The latter is currently marked as 'N6377' and recently moved from Booker to Stow Maries.

Non-flying replicas in the UK include the example at Brooklands Museum, which is painted to represent 'B7270' – the 209 Sqn aircraft Captain Roy Brown was flying when officially credited with downing Baron Manfred von Richthofen. This replica was built in 1977 as G-BFCZ for the Leisure Sport collection but has been at Brooklands since 1988. It is now powered by an original 1916 Clerget rotary engine and is regularly ground run.

The replica Camel at the Fleet Air Arm Museum also served with the Leisure Sport collection (as G-AWYY) although it was actually

built by Slingsby Aviation in 1969 for a Biggles movie that was never filmed. It now carries the markings of 'B6401.'

Elsewhere in the world a great many Camels have been built as either flyable 'warbirds' or museum exhibits, the latter including a highly authentic example built to original drawings for the National Museum of the United States Air Force in Dayton, Ohio. This aircraft is marked as the Camel flown by Lt George A Vaughn Jr while flying with the 17th Aero Squadron.

▲ Among the Camels on display overseas is B7547 at the Royal Army and Military History Museum in Brussels. It is one of around 50 Camels that was in service with the Aviation Militaire between 1917 and 1922 and retains its original Belgian markings. *Steve Bridgewater*

Pups

Today four original Pups remain extant – two of which are regularly flown. Of the static examples, N5182 was built at Kingston upon Thames in 1916 with an 80hp Le Rhône engine. It was allocated to 1 Wing RNAS in September of that year and sent to Dunkirk, France. It performed its first recorded flight on September 8 when Lt E R Grange flew it for 2 hours 25 minutes escorting Sopwith 1½ Strutters on a reconnaissance flight over the Ostend area.

Post war it was stored in France until 1959 when it was were discovered by Lt Cdr Desmond

▲ In addition to the Shuttleworth Collection's Pup/Dove (illustrated on page 3) the only original Pup flying in the world is Roy Palmer's N6161/G-ELRT. The original aircraft force landed behind enemy lines on February 1, 1917 and was captured intact and flown by the Germans for evaluation purposes. Some original items were later retained by a museum and over the last few years these have been combined with other original Sopwith items to reconstruct N6161. The work was done by Retrotec and the aircraft flew again on October 17, 2016. *Steve Bridgewater*

St Cyrien MBE in the Musée de l'Air's reserve collection. He acquired the remains and registered it – appropriately – as G-APUP before restoring it to fly. It flew again in August 1973 but was sold to Doug Arnold's Warbirds of Great Britain Collection in 1979. Three years later he exchanged it with the RAF Museum (receiving Spitfire XVI RW386 in return) and it was on display at Hendon, London until 2015 when it moved to the museum's outpost at Cosford, Shropshire.

Mr St Cyrien later restored a second Pup. N5195 was acquired in the 1960s after 40 years storage in Lincoln area and flew again in 1985 as G-ABOX. Today that combat veteran aircraft can be found as a static exhibit at the Museum of Army Flying at Middle Wallop, Hampshire.

Other than remnants and collections of parts only two other original Pups are thought to survive in their complete form. B1807 was built in 1917 by the Standard Motors Company of Coventry. Following the Great War it was sold and re-registered as G-EAVX. The last time it flew was in the 1921 Aerial Derby at Hendon, where it crashed and thought to have been destroyed. However, in 1972 the remains were found in a barn in Somerset and since that time it has undergone a slow restoration back to flight.

The most recent Pup to return to the skies was Roy Palmer's N6161; a 1916-built example that was delivered to France and force landed on February 1, 1917. The aircraft was captured intact and flown by the Germans for evaluation purposes. Some original items were later retained by a museum and over the last few years these have been combined with other original Sopwith items to reconstruct N6161. The work was done by Retrotec and, registered G-ELRT, the aircraft flew again on October 17, 2016.

Ironically, perhaps the best known of the surviving 'Pups' is not actually a Pup at all. The Shuttleworth Collection's G-EBKY was actually built as a two-seat Dove in 1919. Richard Shuttleworth found it in the mid-30s being flown from a field at Kempston, west of Bedford, by

▲ Replica Camel G-BPOB was built for Frank Tallmantz in the 1970s and was subsequently imported into the UK by Bianchi Aviation Film Services at Booker. The warner Scarab radial engined aircraft is currently marked as RNAS 'N6377' and on based at Stow Maries airfield in Essex. *Darren Harbar*

Geoff Chamberlain. The aircraft had no Certificate of Airworthiness and so the owner was not interested in a legal sale so a deal was done to swap the Dove for an Avro 504K. He the set about restoring the Dove to Pup configuration and it has been based at Old Warden ever since. From 2004 it has been painted to represent '9917', a Beardmore built aircraft which was fitted with Le Prieur Rockets when it served for a time aboard HMS *Manxman*, a seaplane carrier.

Although G-EBKY is thought to be the only surviving 'Dove' a replica of the two-seat version of the Pup was built in the 1990s. Constructed by Skysport Engineering at Hatch, Bedfordshire the 80hp Le Rhône rotary powered aircraft carries the registration G-EAGA that was originally allocated to a Dove that was sold abroad in May 1919. Today it is owned by Andrew Wood and based at Old Warden.

A number of replica Pups have also been constructed around the world, including examples produced in New Zealand by TVAL.

Tabloids & Strutters

Although none of the 43 Sopwith Tabloids or 136 Schneiders survive today the UK is graced with two high quality replicas. One of which, the wheeled variant, was built in the 1970s and first flew (registered G-BFDE) in 1980. Following a landing accident two years later it was sold to the RAF Museum and was on display at Hendon until 2014 when it was placed into storage.

The second example depicts the floatplane that won the 1914 Schneider Trophy and was commissioned by the Kingston Aviation Heritage Trust for the Brooklands Museum.

Even though around 4,500 Sopwith 1 ½ Strutters were built in France and a further 1,439

were constructed in Britain just four original aircraft remain.

Two of these are located in France with No. 556 on display at the Musée de l'air et de l'Espace (Air & Space Museum) in Paris and No. 2897 flying with the Memorial Flight collection at La Ferte Alais. The latter was restored in 2012 and is now the world's sole airworthy Strutter.

Elsewhere, Strutter S85 can be found on display in Belgium as part of the awe-inspiring Brussels Air Museum collection and former Argentinian Air Force '1928' is believed to be

1: The RAF Museum's Triplane was produced in 1917 as N5912. After RFC and RAF service it passed through various hands before being donated to the Imperial War Museum in 1924. After restoration by RAF volunteers it was displayed variously at venues until it moved to the newly created RAF Museum at Hendon in 1971. *RAFM*
2: Strutter 2897 was restored by the Memorial Flight collection at La Ferte Alais in 2012 and is now the world's sole airworthy example of the breed. *Neil Harris*
3: There are numerous flyable replica Pups across the globe – but perhaps none as eye catching as Steve Culp's example. N329CC is fully aerobatic and powered by a Russian 360hp Vedeneyev radial engine!
Steve Bridgewater
4: Brooklands Museum's Sopwith Tabloid replica depicts the floatplane that won the 1914 Schneider Trophy and was commissioned by the Kingston Aviation Heritage Trust for the Brooklands Museum. It is displayed in a half covered configuration to demonstrate the type's construction techniques. *Darren Harbar*
5: A number of non-flying replica Strutters exist around the globe, including this static aircraft built for the 2006 film *Flyboys*. It is now on display in the RAF Manston History Museum. *Key Collection*
6: Replica Dove G-EAGA was constructed by Skysport Engineering at Hatch, Bedfordshire and in the 1990s and is powered by an 80hp La Rhône rotary engine. Today it is owned by Andrew Wood and based at Old Warden. *Steve Bridgewater*

The Shuttleworth Collection's replica Triplane (G-BOCK) was built entirely by volunteer members of Northern Aeroplane Workshops to original plans. On seeing the quality and accuracy of the workmanship Sir Thomas Sopwith declared it to be a late production aircraft rather than a replica! *Darren Harbar*

resembles the real thing the construction methods include a steel tube fuselage.

Triplanes

Just two original Sopwith Triplanes remain extant today – one in the UK and one in Russia.

The RAF Museum's example was produced in 1917 as N5912 and although it didn't see active service it flew with the RFC and RAF as a training aircraft until 1919. The aircraft then passed through various hands before being donated to the Imperial War Museum in 1924. It was stored in the basement in poor condition until it was disposed of in 1932. Four years later the remains were discovered on a dump and it was restored by RAF volunteers. It was displayed variously at the Science Museum and Fleet Air Arm Museum until 1971 when it finally went on exhibition at the newly created RAF Museum at Hendon.

The second survivor, N5486, was sent to the Russian Government in 1917 for evaluation. Fitted with skis, it was later captured by the Bolshevists and used as a trainer in the Red Air Force.

Today the aircraft is on display at the Central Air Force Museum in Monino in what appears to be largely original condition, although the cowling and undercarriage are replacements. In recent years it has been repainted into a bright blue scheme.

A trio of flyable Triplane replicas are active in 2017, including two based in the UK. The Shuttleworth Collection's G-BOCK was built entirely by volunteer members of Northern Aeroplane Workshops to original plans and delivered to Old Warden in June 1990. On seeing the quality and accuracy of the workmanship Sir Thomas Sopwith declared it to be a late production aircraft rather than a replica! Power comes from an original 130hp Clerget rotary engine. It now represents 'N6290'/*Dixie II* of 8 Naval Squadron.

⌃ The RAF Museum has a composite Snipe on display. Although much of it is classed as a replica it does contain elements of various Snipes, including E6655. The elements were assembled in New Zealand by the TVAL team and it arrived in the UK in 2012. *RAF Museum*

under restoration in New Zealand for TVAL. The remains of the ex-Argentinian machine were acquired from US-collector Kermit Weeks in 2011.

A number of airworthy and non-flying replicas also exist around the globe, including a static aircraft built for the 2006 film *Flyboys* (now on display in the RAF Manston History Museum), a flyable replica under construction at the Scottish Museum of Flight at East Fortune and a former flyable replica now at the RAF Museum at Cosford. The latter was built to original Sopwith factory drawings and flown in 1980. It bears the markings of 'A8226', which was initially allotted to the RFC in April 1917 and flew with 45 Sqn. The original A8226 was shot down by Max Ritter von Müller of Jagdstaffel 28 as his thirteenth combat victory.

Further afield the Canadian-based Great War Flying Museum's replica Strutter C-FSOP was built in 2004 to plans produced by Replicraft. It is finished to represent Strutter No. 9739 flown by RNAS Flt Sub Lt Redpath and while it closely

John Brander's replica Triplane (G-BWRA) is one of the most commonly seen aircraft on the UK airshow 'circuit.' Painted to represent the prototype Triplane (N500) it is powered by a Warner Scarab radial engine and is one of the key members of the Great War Display Team. *Steve Bridgewater*

Sopwith

Although built as a less accurate rendition John Brander's G-BWRA is one of the most commonly seen aircraft on the UK airshow 'circuit.' Painted to represent the prototype Triplane (N500) it is powered by a Warner Scarab radial engine and is one of the key members of the Great War Display Team. The aircraft actually began life in the 1970s as a two-seat replica built by John Penny and registered G-PENY.

Further afield replica Triplane ZK-SOP flies in New Zealand as part of the TVAL collection. Construction of this radial engined aircraft began in the USA with Chad Willie but was purchased by the 1914-18 Aviation Trust and shipped to New Zealand in 2007 to be completed by TVAL. The aircraft now flies as N533 *Black Maria*, as flown by Raymond Collishaw of 10 Naval Squadron in July 1917.

▲ Triplane replica ZK-SOP flies in New Zealand as part of the TVAL collection. The aircraft now flies as 'N533' *Black Maria*, as flown by Raymond Collishaw of 10 Naval Squadron in July 1917. *TVAL/Gavin Conroy*

Snipes

Although more than 1,500 Snipes were built in the latter months of the Great War just two examples have survived, along with a replica which incorporates original parts.

Both of the originals are based across the Atlantic with E8105 at the National Air and Space Museum (NASM) in Washington DC and E6938 on display at the Canada Aviation and Space Museum.

E8105 was built in August 1918, by the Ruston Proctor company of Lincoln and after the war was sold to the USA as a private aircraft. In 1951 the aircraft was acquired by Cole Palen for his Old Rhinebeck Aerodrome Museum near New York and he flew it until 1966 when it was damaged in a forced landing. It was later restored as a static exhibit and in 1987 Palen lent it to the NASM. Following his death in 1994, the Snipe was donated to the museum, where it remains today.

E6938 was one of 100 built by Nieuport and General – none of which were delivered until after the Armistice. It served with 37 Sqn before being sold to a former RFC pilot who was working in Hollywood as an actor. He shipped the aircraft to the USA where it was used for ground shots in Howard Hughes' film *Hells Angels*. It then passed through various museums until 1964 when it joined the museum

in Canada and was restored to fly. It was retired in 1970 and has been a museum exhibit ever since.

Interestingly another Snipe relic resides in Canada – the fuselage of William Barker's E8102. This is the aircraft he was flying when he was awarded the Victoria Cross.

In the UK the RAF Museum has a composite Snipe on display. Although much of it is classed as a replica it does contain elements of various Snipes, including E6655. The elements were assembled in New Zealand by the TVAL team and it arrived in the UK in 2012.

In recent years there has been a resurgence in the number of airworthy Snipe replicas thanks to the efforts of TVAL. In addition to the RAF Museum's example the company has now produced three flyable new-build Snipes, one of which ('E8102') resides in Florida with collector Kermit Weeks, one ('F2367') is based at Stow Maries in Essex and one ('E7643') remains with the TVAL collection in New Zealand.

Other Survivors

There are no complete surviving examples of the Sopwith Dolphin but the RAF Museum's 'reproduction' includes a great many original parts that were acquired from Personal Plane Services at Booker in 1967. These included a fuel tank, radiators, bulkhead section, wheels, struts

▲ There are now complete surviving examples of the Sopwith Dolphin but the RAF Museum's 'reproduction' includes a great many original parts. It carries the data plate from Dolphin C3988 and restoration was completed in February 2012. *RAFM*

and tail fin.

A start-stop restoration took place in the 1970s but in 1977 a fuselage section was acquired and this included the data plate from Dolphin C3988. Work on the project did not start in earnest until 1997 and it was not completed until February 2012.

Elsewhere, a replica Dolphin was built at Old Rhinebeck near New York for collector Cole Palen in the 1970s. Registered N47166 and powered by a 150hp Hispano-SSuiza engine, it first flew in 1977 but crashed in 1990 following engine failure. It is currently approaching the end of a lengthy rebuild/restoration. Once complete it will be the only flying representative of the type.

The final surviving 'original' Sopwith aeroplane in this brief survey is the sole remaining example of the Sopwith Baby. The aircraft is marked as 'N2078' but is actually formed from the components of two different Babies – neither of which is N2078! The remains of Babies Nos. 8214 and 8215 have been combined into the composite, which was completed and placed on display at the Fleet Air Arm Museum at Yeovilton in 2016.

With several other examples of classic Sopwith aircraft surviving in component form and the current level of interest in Great War-era aircraft the possibility of at least a few long forgotten airframes emerging as complete aircraft in the years to come. Sopwith may have ceased trading almost a century ago, but the spirit remains strong. ❖

▲ TVAL has so far built three flyable Snipe replicas in New Zealand. One now resides in the UK, one is based in Florida and the third ('E7643') remains with the TVAL collection in New Zealand. *TVAL/Gavin Conroy*